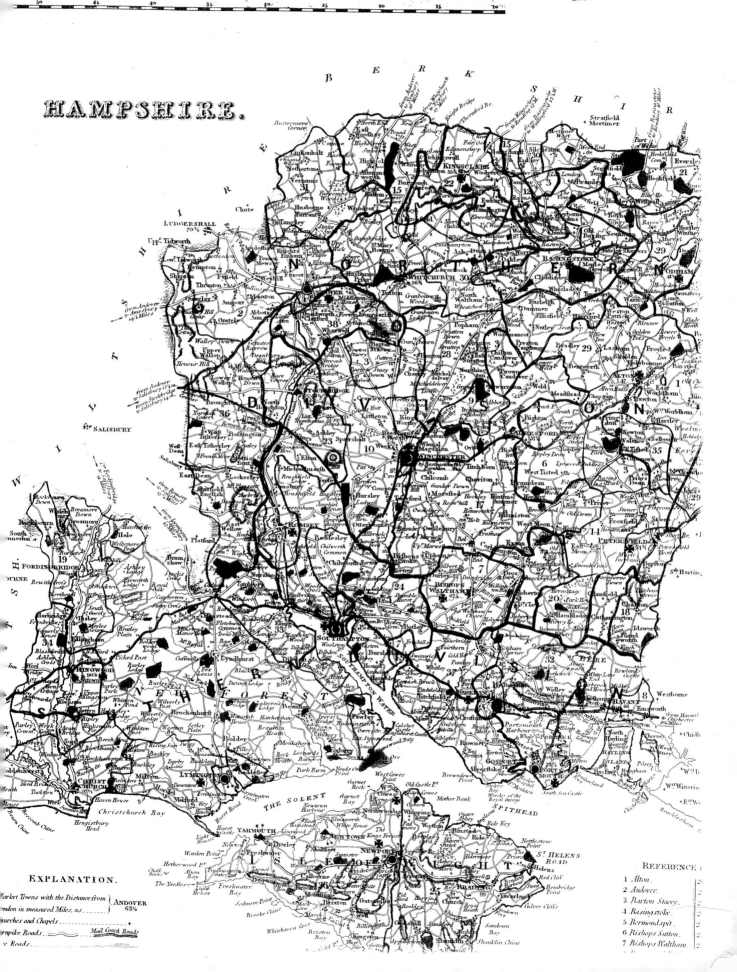

# HAMPSHIRE.

REFERENCE

1 Alton.
2 Andover.
3 Barton Stacey.
4 Basingstoke.
5 Bermondspit.
6 Bishops Sutton.
7 Bishops Waltham.

THE NATIONAL TRUST AND ENGLISH HERITAGE

IN

LONDON AND THE SOUTH EAST

LONDON  SURREY  KENT  SUSSEX  BERKSHIRE

BUCKINGHAMSHIRE  THE ISLE OF WIGHT  HAMPSHIRE

OXFORDSHIRE

185562351X

2002

ARUNDEL CASTLE.
Sussex.

The Seat of his Grace the Duke of Norfolk.

ENGLISH HERITAGE

## ABINGDON COUNTY HALL

In the centre of this desperately busy, rich and active
town right by Oxford, is the historic 17th century County Hall,
built by what was even then a rich town as the courthouse for
the assizes - the precursors of the crown courts.  It stands on
tall columns  with open arcading below so that market traders
could use it (and help out town income from rents), and became
famous for appearing in various TV programmes including the
Ronnie Corbett one of SORRY  in the 1970s and 1980s .   Rather
quieter times too !  I first knew it in the 1970s when the
town museum occupied the upper room.  Well worth seeing
if you can park !

## APPULDURCOMBE

Now with resident falconry centre next door, this is the grandest
Isle of Wight mansion though largely roofless or windowless.
It occupies rising land across from Wroxall and is set in the
unprepossessing grasslands close to Ventnor - it is not the
nicest of places and much poor housing detracts from the
scenery.  The Worsleys had a house here in Tudor times, replaced
wholly in  the early 18th century and remodelled into the
present large classical mansion in the later 18th century.
Fine set of cellars, spooky and forbidding; one restored
room and an exhibition too.  It is charmingly under-commercialised
and quiet, but the children will not be that enthusiastic and
will prefer the donkeys up the road !

BATTLE ABBEY

A most picturesque and historic town greets you when visiting
this seminal place in English history, though it is almost
impossible to cross the road and the parking is dreadful, and
thousands of people clog the place throughout the year and
speak many languages ! When we last went there was a black out
and all the cafes shut down !  The first impression of the abbey
on the site of the Battle of Hastings provides a massive
gatehouse of the sort much in favour in the 1340s  - built
for strength and show, and packed with interest today with its
exhibition etc.  Attached to it is a Tudor, post Reformation,
wing, again impressive, and used as courthouse for the town
at the feet of the abbey then owned by lay masters.

In the distance the private Victorian mansion, built in keeping
with the stone castellated surroundings, and used as a private
school these days.  Beyond and to the left are the abbey ruins,
a great house of Benedictines dating from the 1070s when
William the Conqueror  founded it in order to gloss over the
terrible slaughter of the 1066 battle next door.  The chief
ruin is the dormitory,  formerly the east range of the cloisters
attached to the ruined church: plenty to poke around in, and
much of it built into the mansion next door.  The Victorian
mansion incorporates the monastic buildings plus a Tudor
house built from them.  Lots of space and surprisingly quiet
compared with the gatehouse.

Follow the walk round to enjoy the battlefield.

Places are marked out, such as the spot where Harold of
England died, and the land lies fallow as meadow and odd trees:
a fairly gentle slope downards from the English position to
the  flatter part pccupied by the Normans.   Not that telling
or fascinating without its history, and a small slope and
hill    too !

Lots of pleasure in walking round the mainly undisturbed site
and ruins, and on top of the precinct wall looking over to the
road and town beyond.  The market place is at the abbey gateway
too.

All well cared     for of course, but not THAT impressive
many might say.

## BRAMBER CASTLE

Boxgrove is rather trapped between the busy A27 skirting the
coast just out of Chichester, and the main but quiet A285
swinging north towards Petworth and some very special wooded
hills that form the Downs.  It is a pretty and small place,
with an important medieval church and the ruined monastery.
The house  of Benedictine monks was a creation of the early
12th century and some of the remains are of that date.
Unusually the monastic buildings  seem to have been on the north
side of the church (presumably due to constraints of the site)
and chief remnants are the  guesthouse  and east range of the
cloisters.

The church survives  in use today, an important late Norman
creation into Early English styles and mixing the 2 to create
a handsome whole.  It seems to be  of the period between
1160 and 1220, with a low central tower, plus unusual late
medieval room as porch.  Charming and rather more of
interest than the ruins.

## BRAMBER

Follow the river Adur north from Shoreham and the unloveliness
of the coastal towns and you come to the split in the road
where a right turn takes you along the A2037 with the road looping
round the site of Bramber castle.  Nothing can describe the
horror that my children felt at hearing of the famous
taxidermist Potter and his museum (they having seen some of the
exhibits over the years !) and the lovely village has his monsters
in a museum.  The castle is rather  nicer.

There remains a spectacular mound or motte,  with a small
mound on that, and then a tower keep in ruins but not far short
of 80 feet and suggesting that this was a massive
castle in Norman times when they took over a Saxon fortified
position.  It was largely destroyed in the 1640s but remains
handsome and set in some fine countryside.

BAYHAM OLD ABBEY

We have now tried twice to get into this ruined house of
Premonstratensian canons and failed on both occasions since,
unaccountably, it was closed !  A fair amount of the church,
gatehouse and cloister buildings remain standing though
ruined, and the whole picturesque site was used in the
18th century landscaping of the parkland by the famous
Repton.  He incorporated the abbey ruins into his lovely
landscaping plan with the house beyond the lake, today a
private Victorian mansion.  The monastery is nicely secreted
away from the roads, traffic and so on and is the chief
monastic ruin of the county.

BISHOP'S WALTHAM PALACE

This ruined palace is on the south side of the growing
village of the same name, pleasant rural retreat for the
commuters of Southampton and district and right by the Meon
valley and close to the South Downs and New Forest.  The
ruins are extensive and bear witness to the vastness of the
households  of the Winchester clergy and to their wealth in
creating and maintaining the place.

There may have been an ancient palace on the site before the
total rebuild by  Henry of Blois in the 1130s, when as bishop of
Winchester he spent lavishly for his own use and that of his
clergy and servants as they toured the huge and important
diocese - then number 3 after Canterbury and York, though of
course  Winchester had been capital of Saxon England until
the Normans gave it joint status with London.  After the
more settled times post-Stephen and under Henry II, the palace
was rebuilt in the later 12th century, and  after regular
updates the whole was rebuilt by the influential Bishop
Langton in early Tudor times to create a huge stately pile.

The palace then remained in episcopal use into the Civil
Wars of the 1640s when  it was damaged and never repaired, and
presumably lost much of its stone and roof to the adjoining
town centre .

Huge site and lots to see including an exhibition in repaired
buildings - moat,  great hall, kitchens, tower, chapel, and
interesting use of brick with stone.  A most interesting
spot to spend a few hours.

CARISBROOKE CASTLE

One of the pleasures of my holiday in July 1960 was to
see Carisbrooke, of which I had heard from the book THE
MOONSTONE, with a swashbuckling performance from Stewart
Grainger in a recent film of that name - all pirates, evil,
smuggling and revenge !  So it is a special place, a great
castle full of royal connection, but homely enough with its
donkeys, fine cafe, exhibitions, chapel and shop, extensive
car parking and magnificent views from all parts including
the battlements .Yes, the donkeys remain situ working on
pulling up the water, and the huge earthworks and parade ground
look splendidly green !

It was the key to controlling the island, and had been a
Saxon fortress before the Norman established that large low
keep and incorporated Saxon masonry into it.  The keep today
offers a testing climb up, followed by an equally testing but
more nerve racking walk round the  battlements of the Norman
outer wall: not one way, often exposed to high winds, it is a
miracle nobody gets  blown off or falls off !  You enter the
whole ensemble through a great 14th century gatehouse with
those remarkable rounded twin towers (housing interesting
bits and pieces as well as jackdaws) and then turn right into
the shop before emerging past the  largely early 20th
century chapel (on medieval base) before meeting the great
courtyard with its newly created garden, lots of toilets, and
in the distance the keep and the exhibitions and cafe below it
on the steep slopes.

The Redvers family owned the castle into the 1290s when
Edward Ist - arch castle builder of Wales etc - bought it
and the place stayed royal.

The donkey accommodation is excellent and newish, and they trot
across to the well house occasionally for a bit of light
exercise: be warned, you have to queue for ages when busy,
and it is not that exciting to see a donkey in a treadmill
winding up a bucket of water from 180 feet down !  Novel, but
when you have seen it once ...  It also gets highly
claustrophobic in there with 200 others !

The chief stone building not in ruins is like a manor house,
and was much rebuilt in the mid Victorian years for a daughter
of Queen Victoria.  The result is a fine tall and imposing
building, packed with interest as museum, but dark - well worth
2 looks to see what you missed first time.

King Charles Ist was prisoner here a year or more in 1648,
trying to escape  to France before being finally taken to
London and his death.   It gets very busy and foreigners
love it.  Old pictures will show you have it all used to
look: Newport has grown to its gates almost, but the
rural feel remains and the quaint traffic lights
controlling access are those of 1960 - without an amber and
no timing !

## THE CONDUIT HOUSE

 Waterworksbuilding for the water supply some distance from
the abbey of St Augustine in Canterbury: not that telling these
days when viewed, more of a curiosity and rare survival.

## DEAL CASTLE

One of the great chain of forts along the south coast, Deal
castle sits on the sea front of the modern and expanding town
and resort: I approached from the landward side in heavy rain
and did not realise that the  entrance is modest and in no way
prepares you for the size of the seward fort .  A central
rounded keep is surrounded by  2 rings of semi circular bastions,
forming a symmetrical defensive plan for maximum defence from
artillery but providing cannons  within the maximum angle and
range for firing.  It was state of the art 1540s, one of the
largest, and a key player in case of French invasion.

In the 17th century it became more of a residence and
by the 18th century the post of captain or warden was honorary
and provided a fine seaside home for some dignitary or minor
royal.  Lots of spooky passageways, major cellar or
basement , imposing battlements, but no garden  - just grass and
views.  It has been restored back to its Tudor origins.

## CALSHOT CASTLE

The best view of this small round and low-built fort is  out in
the Solent, entering Southampton Water from the Isle of Wight
opposite, but you need to know where to look : the castle is
a small fort of late Tudor times, built to defend the vulnerable
south coast with a string of others.  In immaculate shape,
the fort lies on a spit of land close to Fawley (the great
oil refinery), and was in use for military purposes into
fairly recent times.   Low and rounded and thickly walled,
Calshot was aimed at artillery defence of the Water
and to provide a poor target in turn.

## CAMBER CASTLE

Camber is best known for its motley settlement strung out along
the coast south of Rye - and fairly down market one local told
me ! - with the well known Camber Sands: but it also has a
ruined castle across the river Rother after it spills down
from Rye to the north and enters the sea.  Originally this was
a c1540 late Tudor fort built for canon to protect the
town and  port as it then was, and it had the sea right up
against its walls .  It is now over a mile from the sea but
it does have various lakes or ponds left between   the 2.
Though typical of its type it is important for never having been
updated or uprated over the next 550 years.  Good walking
around the nature reserve which surrounds it these days on the
reclaimed land.

DEDDINGTON CASTLE

An expanding village setting for commuters to Oxford, not that
far from the Cotswolds, is home to a very large series of
earthworks defences once with castle and curtain walling.
Nothing remains to see save the view and mounds - the lot was
demolished in the 14th century and presumably re-used.

DONNINGTON CASTLE

On a spur of rising land is the majestic gatehouse of the
        castle of Donnington: plenty of earthworks but
nothing much else thanks to the Civil Wars of the 1640s and
the ferocious fighting centring on the castle.  Splendid
reminder of times past and formerly controlling the Bath road.

DOVER CASTLE

Remember that Dover castle is one of the major monuments of the
nation: it is truly vast, requiring much energy to view it, and
gets horridly busy with mostly overseas folk who do not come
as families but always in coach loads !   You have been
warned !

Sited toweringly above the town, harbour and coast, the castle
occupies a site used by Iron Age folk, then by the Romans and
with a huge lighthouse or pharos dating from Roman times and
used to guide boats across from the continent.  Earthworks
are ancient and formidable.  Not much left of the Norman
castle c1070, but Henry IInd strengthened the lot and put up a
great keep which remains to be explored if you can climb the
hill to its massive set of steps !  All added to c1220 after
the civil wars of King John's time, and especially improved c
1800 against the French and in the 20th century twice against
the Germans.

Below the keep is a huge system of tunnels dug into the chalk
and originally of the 1200s before various extensions, and still
in use during the last war.  Underground too the HQ for Winston
Churchill and his hundreds of helpers in the last war, and
all recreated in the 1990s for visitors : again it is huge

so pace yourself !    Barracks, courtyards on the flat, then a stiff walk to various curtain walls, earthworks, gatehouse, wide grounds, fabulous views and the big church of St Mary de Castro and right by the pharos.  Roman brickwork and Saxon masonry make this an important place, and the experts often attend to explore both.  Very impressive too.

It had an exhibition devoted to Henry VIII and his visit here in  1539 to oversee improvements in the face of the  French invasion threat.  A magnificent site and sight.

## FLOWERDOWN

Round barrows or  earthworks just out of Winchester and used as a Bronze age burial site.

## FORT BROCKHURST

Set on some open land north of the great urban district that is Gosport is this fort,a survivor from the string of such defences built round Portsmouth Harbour in the 1850s when there was a fear of French or other invasion, and marking the end of such places that had commenced in Roman times.  Huge earthworks and moat, stone defences, and state of the art c1860 provision for artillery to defend  the home of the Royal navy into the 20th century.  Splendid keep now in use for functions I was told.

## FORT CUMBERLAND

Set in the Eastney part of Portsmouth is this imposing and large late 18th and early 19th century fort.  I have never found it open to view.

## HORNE'S PLACE CHAPEL

A rarely seen small property is this 14th century chapel for the attached manor house in this Kent village about 2 miles from the village of Appledore.  It was licensed for services in the 1360s, and in 1381 the property was attacked in the great Wat Tyler rebellion of that year.

## HURST CASTLE

Take to a ferry at Keyhaven or walk the fair distance along
a footpath on top of the spit of sand, dune and pebble that
supports this key castle set low and menacingly guarding the
narrow west entry to the Solent and therefore Portsmouth and
Southampton.  In bad weather it is remote and spooky, not the
sort of place to stay overnight in.  It was built by Henry VIII
in the 1530s panic against the French and is one of the
larger of its type thanks to extensive rebuilding in the 19th
and 20th century emergencies.  Good view of it  from the IOW
ferries etc.

## PORTSMOUTH'S KING JAMES'S AND LANDPORT GATES

Two great gates  which formerly gave access through the huge
defensive walls of the city of Portsmouth.  Most were demolished
in Victorian times: St James's is of 1687 and has had several
sites; Landport remains in situ, the only one left, dated 1760.
Both impressive monuments but you only seem to see the outside,
they being in sensitive areas for security.

## KIT'S COTY HOUSE AND LITTL  KIT'S COTY HOUSE

  The former is near Aylesford in Kent, and is a megalithic
burial chamber originally covered by a long barrow about 200
feet long.  The latter is 500 yards away and is basically a
damaged similar tomb.

## KNIGHTS TEMPLAR CHURCH

The fairly uninformative  stone foundations of a church of the
Order of the Knights Templars on the hill above Dover.

## LULLINGSTONE ROMAN VILLA

The village is lucky - just out of the big towns and London,
but with a castle, nice houses and above all the famous villa
dating from the later 1st century AD, and not that long after
the Romans brought their way of life to Kent and the district
between Orpington and Rochester.

It shows today a complex cycle of growth and decay over a period
of 4 centuries, and has not only famous mosaics but also
one of the first Christian chapels (of about 360AD) which replaced
the special worship room previously created along the lines
of other villas of the wealthy Romano-British upper classes.
A splendid example of how to best show off an ancient
monument.

## MAISON DIEU, OSPRINGE NEAR FAVERSHAM

Just off the busy A2 is the half timbered medieval Maison Dieu or
house of God, it being part of a complex of medieval buildings
forming royal lodge, almshouses or hospital and hospital itself.
Picturesque and well worth a view.

## THE MEDIEVAL MERCHANT'S HOUSE, SOUTHAMPTON

Splendid example of a rich merchant's house of the 1290s,
with Edward Ist at his peak,  and the Fortin family building
this house with storage cellars for their trade with
Bordeaux.  Very atmospheric and nicely kitted out these days:
small rear yard and some desperate housing round about, but
a joy to explore its dark interior on this deep plot.   We have
been twice without meeting anyone else.

## MILTON CHANTRY, NEAR GRAVESEND, KENT

Quite hard to find this diminutive building in Fort Gardens,
a rare survival of a 14th century chapel for the leper
hospital and including a tiny family chantry for the souls of
the dead.  It was later on  a piece of both a fort and a pub:
it being an early stop into the Thames from abroad, it was the
sort of hospital where one dropped one's lepers off before going
into London.

## MINSTER LOVELL

In the 40 odd years that I have known this spot in Oxfordshire it
has grown substantially.  The old core of the charming and ancient
village retains the handsome Cotswold inn where my father and
I would dine and luncheon in a leisured era, and then we would
walk down to the ruined hall of the once great Lovell family
who came to grief in the 1480s thanks to oppsoing Henry Tudor
when their own star was in  the ascendant.   Handsome setting
though too close to Witney  these days !

NORTH HINKSEY CONDUTI HOUSE

In North HInksey close to Oxford is this roofed reservoir which
housed the first water main pipes for the city of Oxford and
dating from Jacobean times c1610.  An unusual creation.

NORTH LEIGH ROMAN VILLA

10 miles out of Oxford is the village of North Leigh with its
famous church, the handsome river Evenlode, and the Roman villa:
not especially interesting compared with the presentation of
some such villas, but this one does have a famous mosaic
floor (tile mosaics) in various shades of red and brown.
 Well worth a viewing.

NORTINGTON GRANGE

Set in the wooded landscape north of New Alresford and
Winchester in Hampshire is this splendid pile.  It was used in
one of those Russian based films - EUGENE ONEGIN I recall - as
backcloth, looking severe and wintry enough to appear in
St Petersburg.  It is an early and important Greek Revival
mansion in handsome parkland, but you have to view from
outside.  It was built in the early 1800s around a 17th
century mansion for the banking Drummond family.

OLD SOAR MANOR

Close to PLaxtol in Kent is this intriguing part of a
13th century manor house, stone and the solar end of the former
house - the old hall site is built on with a Georgian house,
strangely enough.  Nice chapel of 1290 or so and a pleasing
place.

OSBORNE HOUSE

I first viewed this great house near Cowes on the Isle of Wight
in 1960 and have gone back regularly.  IN recent years the old
nursing home part for civil servants et al seems to have gone,
and no longer do you see their wheel chairs hairing down the
paths !  The whole vast building has been done up in the
yellow of its original colour; the walled gardens and lawns,
new flower beds and paths are immaculately kept; and you get
free rides on the horse drawn carriages.

Queen Victoria bought the old small Georgian house and large
estate running down to the Solent in 1845 as a summer
home for her children, and the new great house was built
by 1851 to designs by the London developer and builder Thomas
Cubitt who had come to the attention of Prince Albert.

It comprises an original L shaped mansion with 2 great towers,
with a large wing of the 1890s (the Durbar Wing), the whole
surrounded by extensive gardens and grounds, a rising site
sloping down to private beach on the Solent facing Portsmouth,
and generally  on  a vast scale.  All Italianate in style,
which led to thousands of smaller versions being buildt throughou
Britain !   Miles of corridors, opulent and heavy Victorian
furnishings throughout (so if you do not like such crowded
rich decors this is not for you), plus endless German and
Victorian statues, busts, paintings and so on together with the
usual family paintings.

The Durban Wing is a magnificent  celebration of all things
Indian : Victoria moped for Albert from 1861 until the
1870s when Benjamin Disraeli (worried about republican sympathies
and other problems brought by an absent and invisible queen)
suggested she become empress of India.  Thereafter began her
love affair with that sub-continent with the resultant wing.
Most impressive in every respect, and the queen had a new
enthusiasm.

The grounds have much to see including Italianate architecture
in the  houses and cottages of the estate, plus the strange
and large Swiss Cottage for the children to live in during
playtimes complete with kitchen and some macabre furnishings.

Victoria died here in January 1901 and her son Edward VII
gave the estate to the nation since it was surplus to his
requirements and reminded him too much of his excessively
longlived mother and his father !

Some shade in the car park for dogs and picnics; endless room
to wander; piles of foreign tourist and coaches.  Vast amounts
of money are being spent on the property at the moment,
which is  it is fair to say had not changed much between 1960
and 1997.

## PEVENSEY CASTLE

Set just off the busy A259 near Eastbourne is this massive
castle which was a creation of the Roman defence of the coastal
districts in the late 3rd century, and which remains almost to
its full original height in quite formidable guise - and was
occupied by the Norman in September 1066 before Hastings.
It was considerably strengthened in the middle ages to provide
a strong castle never taken by force, and continued to be
in service  during the 20th century war emergencies.  The chief
remains are Roman with medieval improvements - I was quite
startled by its 10 acre size and high walls lasting more or
less in tact for 1700 years.

## PORTCHESTER CASTLE

At the top of the intensively developed Portsmouth Harbour is
a peninsula of land with this great castle on it, formerly
a vital cog in the Roman defences of the later 3rd century
against the Anglo-Saxons, and  with a Norman castle built on
one side.  It remained the important embarkation gathering
spot for kings throughout the middle ages into the 17th
century.   It remained in use in a limited way into the
19th century as a place for French prisoners of war to be
kept.  It retains its entire fortifications to their
original height and the sea comes right to its base.  It is
another monumental site, hugely impressive and steeped in
history.

## RECULVER TOWERS AND ROMAN FORT

Another Roman fort, but this time largely destroyed by
erosion on the coastal position.  What remains is still impressive
but overshadowed by the  west front and twin towers attached
to  what was an important Norman church.  Most of the site was
cleared  in the 19th century but the twin towers were saved
for use in guiding shipping with their lights.
Hugely impressive.

## RICHBOROUGH ROMAN FORT  AND AMPHITHEATRE

Near Sandwich in Kent, this is a key position in  Roman times
after the landings of 43AD.  Great open theatre site, plus the
remains of the important 6 acres fort with hug walls and bases.
Excellent museum.

# ROCHESTER CASTLE

The critically sited town of Rochester is ancient and formed
a vital part of naval protection for the coast along the Medway
and round to the Thames and London for centuries.  Of the
formerly extensive fortifications only the keep and curtain
walls remain: 70 foot square, 113 feet high, with walls around
12 feet thick, the keep is impressive but sitting in the
charming surrounding park gives no impression of the brutal
fortress that once was.  Henry IInd made William the Conqueror's
castle far stronger,  and the cathedral is nearby - twin pillars
of Norman control.

# THE ROLLRIGHT STONES

These used to take some finding down narrow Oxfordshire
lanes near Chipping Norton, 3 groups of stones handsomely
set in the countryside, often quiet even today: the King's Men,
the Whispering Knights, and the King Stone form the 3 groupings
which span 2000 years of history before the Celts and Romans.
Do not expect Stone Henge, nor the crowds !

# ROYAL GARRISON CHURCH

It did not impress me on the chilly March day when we visited
this ruined chancel part of a medieval church in what remains of
old Portsmouth in Hampshire, but then it is a precious survival
of  a hospice created in the early 13th century for pilgrims
landing by boat to do their journeys.  It was within the new
and huge defences and after being used for storage, became the
garrison's own church until being destroyed in German bombing
(along with most of old Portsmouth) in 1941.

# RYCOTE CHAPEL

15th century chapel in the grounds of a demolished mansion
near Thame in Oxfordshire, and justly famous for its magnificent
furnishings -  fine musicians gallery,  Jacobean pulpit,
15th to 17th century woodwork and 2 great roofed pews which
form quite a centre of interest to show how things were in olden
times.  A gem of a place.

## ST AUGUSTINE'S CROSS

Marking the traditional spot where St Augustine landed
in 597 to convert the Saxons, marked with a cross of 19th
century vintage in the open land near Minster in Kent.
You have to have imagination for this one !


## ST AUGUSTINE'S ABBEY

Surprisingly hard to find in the flat landscape of the
city of Canterbury is this extensive grass plot with fine
tourist centre but only scant remains of the formerly
huge house of Benedictine monks and site of the burial of
St Augustine himself.  It was one of the powerhouses of
Christianity from c600 into the 1530s, and was truly monumental
in size: most of it was torn down for local building
projects including the local college for teaching clergy
in the 19th century.  We visited to find the only others on a
lovely sunny spring day were Japanese tourists !  It is
easily missed out and poorly signposted for pedestrians,
so be warned !  and you need good shoes if it is at all wet.
The ruins are not that telling or informative.


## ST CATHERINE'S ORATORY

High above the village of Niton and Blackgang Chine on the south
east, back of the Wight, coastline is this  14th century pepperpot
lighthouse - small but prominent, and worth the climb to see it
and enjoy the views, and usually quiet.


## ST JOHN'S COMMANDERY

A medieval chapel in the countryside near Densole in Kent,
and converted into a farmhouse after the Dissolution of the
monasteries in the 1530s: I have never been able to get inside
to enjoy the furnishings, but it looks handsome enough in the
sun.


## ST LEONARD'S TOWER

IN THE COUNTRYSIDE OUTSIDE OF WEST MALLING IS THIS most
imposing tower keep of Norman vintage, possibly 1070s and
built by the bishop of Rochester: fine piece of walling too,
and in the same parish remains the formerly large abbey.

SILCHESTER ROMAN WALLS AND  AMPHITHEATRE

Set outside the village of Silchester south of Reading is
the extensive Roman site,  famed for its enormous
amphitheatre and its Roman walls.  An oddly shaped site of
235 acres formed the town  with the usual gates, forum, houses,
businesses and a 4th century Christian church.  Not much to
excite you visually however.


SUTTON VALENCE CASTLE

Near Maidstone in Kent and beautifully situated on the
Wealden escarpment is this small castle ruin, Norman and
pleasant in the evening sun.


TEMPLE MANOR

Pleasantly set in gardens is this remnant of the Order of the
Knights Templar, in Rochester's urban area, and simply a
rebuilt and  handsomely presented farmhouse of 17th century
brick with  a 13th century  building attached.  It was a
nunnery after the suppression of the Order, and after
Dissolution in the 1530s somehow survived to be restored.
It looks rather like an arts and crafts attempt to look
medieval from some angles, and contains  a vaulted undercroft
and great hall.


TITCHFIELD ABBEY

Surprisingly rural given its position hemmed in by the
Fareham to Southampton conurbation is this village with
its  formerly great abbey of  various bits and pieces but
memorable for the vast Tudor gatehouse which  allowed entry
to the great house built  out of the abbey ruins in the
1540s by the earl of Southampton and demolished to form a
picturesque ruin in the 1780s.


UFFINGTON CASTLE, THE WHITE HORSE AND DRAGON HILL

These are prehistoric sites lying along the famous old
Ridgeway  between Swindon and Wantage and now nominally in
Oxfordshire.  Dragon HIll is  a high natural mound in the
downs, with  an extensive iron age camp and  the famous
great white horse cut out of the turf to reveal the chalk.
It is a brilliant Celtic representation of a horse, or
earlier.  Steep climbs abound: wonderful views: surprisingly
busy at times.

## UPNOR CASTLE

The village is overwhelmed by the burgeoning Medway towns
these days, but the castle is a wonderful picture of a fortified
manor house or artillery fort buil in the emergencies of the
1560s to protect the estuary from foreign raiders.  This was
a vital artery in the shipping trade,  but the castle proved
     inadequate in the Dutch raids of the 17th century.   Still
     it is beautifully preserved and splendid looking on the  water.

## WALMER CASTLE

South of increasingly busy and urban Deal is this splendid
remnant of an earlier age, with endless coastal vistas, beach,
some woodland and fairly traffic free.  It is one of the
magnificent line of artillery forts built c1540 in the
emergencies of the late Tudor era by Henry VIII once he had
alienated most of Europe and feared invasion.  It became
official residence  of the Lord Warden of the Cinque Ports and
until 2002 received an annual visit as holiday home for the
Queen Mother in her role as Lord Warden.  Externally there is no
doubting its function, but it  was much altered by successive
Wardens and above all by the Duke of Wellington in the
1830s and 1840s - it retains much of the atmosphere of
a small country house, and is packed with interesting
furnishings chiefly of  Wellington's era.

Lots to see and to enjoy including the splendid gardens which
continue to surprise: quite a focal point for local civic
pride too, and when we went at Easter we were the only
people touring (plus the garden cat).  You could be very
happy and contented here !

## WAVERLEY ABBEY

The  first house of the austere and powerful Cistercian Order of
monks founded in Britain, in the 1120s, and presumably the
powerhouse for the Order and for its architectural
expression - though little remains above ground level so
comprehensively was it destroyed in the 1530s and later and
reused somewhere else.  Lovely spot close to Farnham.

## WAYLAND'S SMITHY

Enjoy this atmospheric Neolithic burial site with its

enfolding trees  in the downland of the Ridgeway.  It
featured in such stories as the Moon POny (on TV 20 odd years ago)
and is part of the vast ancient heritage of the district of the
downs.  Lovely views and walks.


WESTERN HEIGHTS

High above Dover on the coast is this rump of an artillery
fort built against French invasion c1800: nice walking and
viewing.


WOLVESEY PALACE OR CASTLE

Not that far from Winchester cathedral is this famous
ruin.  It was a huge medieval  castle and palace for the bishops
of Winchester - one of the most powerful and wealthiest of
medieval prelates -  and Mary Tudor spent her honeymoon with
Philip IInd of Spain within its luxury in 1554.  It was
trashed by the Parliamentary forces in the 1640s and
charming ruins remain in a fine setting, with old city walls
nearby.


YARMOUTH CASTLE

You tie up beside this Tudor artillery fort with the ferry
beneath its guns on the Isle of Wight.  It houses a pleasant
lawned rooftop garden for picnics but the wind is terrible,
and has unusualy brick-lined rooms and stonework for the
gunpowder etc to be stored.  Small and fascinating with its
old photos upstairs, it is worth an hour or 2 of
anyone's time.

## 26

WESTMINSTER ABBEY

The abbey of course is not part of the deal for EH: they have
instead the chapter house, Pyx chamber and abbey museum in this
incredibly tourist ridden district of London.  The abbey is one
of the very few of cathedral status which has no bishop
involved, and since the 11th century  has played a seminal role
in the affairs of the nation.  The chapter house is the great
meeting house building for the chapter - the canons, minor canons
and so on who run the show.  Each abbey, priory and
cathedral had one befroe the Reformation of the 1530s and
many remain, like this one, a riot of well cared for colour from
the wall  paintings and famous sculptures - as vivid as it
has ever been.   It is also octagonal, as was common for such
buildings, and retains its original glazed tile floor, though the
throngs may diminish its status in your eyes.  The socalled
Pyx chamber or chapel  is 11th century - the chapter house is
mid 13th century so 200 years newer - and also houses
cathedral treasures, as does the large abbey museum.  It takes
time to get in, to view and to savour such a pile of history so
allow plenty of time.   Even in the          winter it gets
busy.


CHISWICK HOUSE


If like us you travel vast distances by train to get to London
then ensure you get a taxi to this spot, set in the wide acres
of the surrounding park and quite hard to find if you are not
local.  Last time we were there it was a park packed with
scores of dogs and thousands of children, with some very
iffy facilities and only toilets at the house itself, so do not
expect to stay too long after viewing.

The house was built in the village of Chiswick, some distance
from the Thames, at a time when this quite  remote from  London.
It dates from the 1720s and is regarded as a magnificent house in
the Palladian style- but what surprised me was how small it all
was compared with the proper stately homes.  The 3rd earl of
Burlington, a cultivated  and cultured wealthy patron, was much
influenced by his continental tours and sought to achieve expression
here of what he had admired in the architect Palladio in
Italy, with the help of William Kent and architect designer.

## 27

The result - repaired after German bomb damage - is a villa
with domed lantern, square     shaped, portico with columns,
complex and detailed stairways and staircases outside,
and a strange looking ground floor squashed beneath the
massive first floor and its dome.  The private library, private
rooms and servants were  on the ground, the public rooms being
the grand ones - vividly decorated and coloured and quite
inspiring to the modern eye.  A beautiful place indeed and
packed with colour   and detail.

## COOMBE CONDUIT

A rarity is this,  2 small Tudor buildings connected by an
underground passage which supplied water to the enormous
Hampton Court Palace in Tudor times when at its greatest
extent and power.   The opening times are seriously
restricted and we have never been able to get into them.  Worth
seeing though.

## DANSON HOUSE

We have not seen this property in Bexley, east London, and assume
it to be a fairly new acquisition.  It is a 3 storey house of
the 1760s built in a mixed Georgian and Palladian style which
produces an oddly sever outline.  It remains undergoing
extensive repairs.

## DOWN HOUSE, DOWNE, KENT

The home of the eminent Naturalist Charles Darwin and his numerous
family in the 19th century, built as a leafY  rural retreat.

## 28

It now      . sits uncomfortably close to the  busy and hectic
roads and towns inside the M25 close to Orpington and
Croydon.  BiggIN  HIll airport is next  door: the oasis to an
extent remains though.

Darwin returned from his epic round the world voyages on  the
BEAGLE - portrayed some years ago very vividly on BBC TV and
in various books - in 1836, decided to live in London and
married his cousin the wealthy Emma Wedgwood of the famous
pottery and porcelain empire.   He felt his health was harmed
in the dirt and disease of the city and with his large
income and increasing numbers of children he removed to
a late 18th century farmhouse , which he extended and
considerably altered.  The house today retains much    its
inte    and furnishings from the 19th century together with
important Darwin collections and  items.

Darwin delayed the publication of his theories on evolutiopn
until 1859, when his youthful supporters pressured      him to
beat rivals to the new science: Darwin of course knew what an
outrage would be created, but he let  younger men fight his
battles aned carried on the quiet family life here.  Down house
is the birthplace of  ON THE ORIGIN OF SPECIEs  BY MEAN    OF
NATURAL SELECTION , but it was also the centre of a happy
and extended family life.  It is a pleasant place to visit -
all the revolutionaries have been quiet unassuming people !

Much restored at vast cost in recent years.


ELTHAM PALACE


In Eltham, south east London, off Court Road in SE9 is this
wonderful place, much improved in recent years and much
publicised by EH.  It is only yards from the busy High St yet
this is the remains of one ofthe nation's largest medieval
royal palaces.   It is also joined literally to one of the
seminal 1930s icons of taste in the form of a house for a very
wealthy family, a double bonus for tourists.  The original
palace was chiefly a 15th century creation embracing major work
by the          Yorkist king Edward IV - he of the evil brother
who allegedly killed the princes, his nephews, in the tower of
London.   Henry VIII was the last of the monarchs to spend much
time here in what was a handy stop on the way to the coast.

## 29

The great hall , incorporated into the 1930s house, was a
creation of the 1470s for royal dining in huge numbers,
but in the 17th and 18th centuries it along with most of
the site decayed and became barns and outbuildings.
It was regularly painted in what was then the rural pleasures of
the district, but it was planned to be demolished in the
1820s and saved after something of a novel campaign was
launched.    It became a huge sitting room in the 1930s for the
new owners.

Enjoy the gardens, the terrace, the moat,  the exhibitions and
so on: my wife's favourite is the 1930s house, designed for
the Courtauld family - millionaires and knowing what they
liked in the French art deco style which has recently
undergone a revival.  Many think it looks like the Cunard ocean
liner style of the era in its spacious opulence yet daring
decoration.

The Courtaulds employed various designers of course, each
producing an expensive but beautiful room or part of the
house   .

The entrance way is via large black and silver doors featuring
London zoo animals and birds, followed by  the dining room,
huge sitting room come great hall, and suites of bedrooms -
vaulted bathroom for the owners with  onyx and gold mosaic,
gold plated bath taps and statue of the goddess Psyche !
And the furniture !  marvellous chairs and tables, wall
decorations and splendid circular rug or carpet which was
specially made recently (in Belfast I think and featured on
TV several times).

The place is a must for tourists and EH have spent a fortune
very wisely.


JEWEL TOWER

IN Abingdon Street near the parliament buildings is one of the
2 surviving buildings of the original palace of Westminster,
built in the 1360s and inevitably much altered since.  It
houses a special parliamentary exhibition at present.  NOte that
one of the problems in this area is the lack of public
loos and the total absence of anything to put rubbish in !
Security is tight and does not cater for children !

KENWOOD

Lying between Highgate and Hampstead, beside Hampstead Heath in north London is this magnificent mansion.  The earl of Mansfield, one of the great judicial influences of any era and lord chancellor (head of the legal system) owned the house and called in Robert Adam in the 1760s and 1770s to remodel entirely the property.  It was a plain brick house transformed into a richly decorated villa and EH have spent a packet on restoring the whole in recent years.

The earl of Iveagh bought the property in the early 20th century to prevent its being built on - he being the millionaire brewer - and then on his death in 1927 it passed to the nation together with some of his vast art and furniture collection.   Thus the famous Iveagh bequest of paintings which graces the house today.

The house is a must : so too the extensive landscaped grounds with their famous lake and the open air concerts with only the performers having any protection from the fickle summer weather -  you sit on the grassy slopes opposite and let the music waft across the lake from the rounded building protecting the  orchestra.  All very civilised indeed !

Much to see and do and very popular indeed.

LONDON WALL

Not too exciting stretch of Roman wall which formed part of the eastern defences for the Roman city of Londinium.   It is a curiosity and is by Tower Hill underground station to greet visitors.

MARBLE HILL HOUSE

Beautifully positioned mansion on the river Thames in a large park setting:is this  one of the most desirable properties in the district ?  It was built about 1730 - and is a good example of the early Georgian style of that era - for the

mistress of George II, Henrietta Howard, countess of
Suffolk.  It was in its day the centre of a magic circle  of
famous people including artists, writers and politicians,
and has once more been lavishly improved and restored by
EH in recent years.  The decor is especially lavish and
entertaining: enjoy the exhibitions, displays and grounds for
this    is a gem.


WELLINGTON ARCH

Famous to millions for its position on Hyde Park Corner is this
triumphal arch, designed in 1825 by the illustrious Decimus Burton
and commissioned by George IV: it was meant to be the
outer entrance for Buckingham Palace along with a second outer
arch come gateway.  Decimus Burton did not design it with the
enormous statue of the duke of Wellington in mind when this
was added, 28 feet high and weighing in at 40 tons !

The arch was removed to its present      position in 1882 and
Wellington's statue removed, replaced by the angel of peace
descending on the chariot of war - it remains the largest
bronze statue in the nation and was unveiled in 1912 (designed
by sculptor Adrian Jones).

It houses rooms with exhibitions in them and presents an
enormous obstacle to views !


WERNHER COLLECTION, THE RANGER'S HOUSE, GREENWICH PArk


Ranger's House is a noble red brick 18th century house on the
edge of Greenwich Park, improved by stone entrance facade and
steps, and by the fine wrought iron railings   which welcome you.
Inside the house is furnished as though a palace, from the
internationally famous and    important collection of Julius
Wernher.  He had come from Germany aged 21 in 1871 and made his

money  in the diamond trade with South Africa, amassing an
enormous fortune which he spent on his art  collection.
He married in 1888, and his wife  Alice Birdie spent his money
for him : lavish lifestyle, endless parties for the very
richest and most powerful in society, and above all in building
a new mansion at Luton HOO to house increasing numbers of
art items purchased from all over the world.

Julius made baronet in 1904 and left £11 million on his      death
in 1912:  Birdie lived on to 1945: they had 3 sons, 1 killed
in the first world war.   The collection was partly dispersed,
but a core remains - old master paintings,  Renaissance jewels,
rare carved ivories,  the best in silver ware and ceramics,
the most expensive of tapestries and furniture and so on.
The collection is used      elswhere too and makes everywhere it
goes look wonderful.


THE STATUES OF LONDON

EH is responsible for the care and upkeep of  47 statues and
monuments in central London - some are huge, all are important,
so enjoy them in their present splendid condition as money is
lavished on them.

NATIONAL TRUST

## 34

## ALFRISTON CLERGY HOUSE

Alongside the river Cuckmere in the valley cutting through the
South Downs and not that far from the sea is this NT
property, a handsome thatched 14th century example of the old
Wealden hall house type. This was the first property purchased
by the NT, in 1896, and is an example of a clergy house - ie
where the medieval clergy would have lived their celibate life,
vicar and rector plus curates and male servants. It is an
utterly picturesque spot, of garden ancient property and
fine neighbours alongside the old church - all very English
and it gets very busy too. The river and its meadows are
enchanting in the spring sunshine, as when we last visited.
Sussex at its finest.


## ASCOTT

This house is part of the substantial legacy of the
Rothschilds, and the Vale of Aylesbury in Buckinghamshire
has for 150 years felt the influence of the family and its money.

Nathan Mayer de Rothschild arrived in England in 1798 from the
continent, something of a refugee from the excesses then being
perpetrated in the French Revolution. He made money in various
enterprises but above all in banking, and his 3 sons -
Mayer, Anthony and Lionel bought up estates in the Vale
from the 1850s. The district was very accessible and not too
distant from London - source of all money - and with the new
railways and roads the family were able to commuite fairly
easily between the 2 - often bringing home to the Vale and
their country pursuits, a host of wealthy and top of the rung
society people. They were about the first to mix business with
pleasure by unleashing princes and the very rich on the English
countryside in pursuit of game.

Mayer bought Mentmore; Anthony, Aston Clinton; Lionel bought
Halton (though the new house was built by his son Alfred).
They bought at a time of falling rural incomes for the rich and
of agricultural depression and got bargains.

The family then bought        properties in the next depression:
Lionel bought Tring Park on the Hertford border in 1872; Mayer
bought Ascott in 1873 and gave it to his nephew Leopold; and
Ferdinand, another     nephew, and from Austria, bought
Waddesdon in 1874. The latter's sister bought the Eythrope estate
in 1876.

## 35

Thus Ascott came to the Rothschilds in 1873 and was used as
a hunting lodge in what was then wild and game-ful country.
It was a small Jacobean timber framed property which then
went through 8 major phases of rebuilding and extension to
create a very substantial mansion, and all given the black and
white feel in and out in the 1930s.  Lovely collection of
paintings and furnishings inside, splendid gardens outside -
money well spent .   Many will recall from their school history
how it was the Rothschilds and their connection   which
helped Disraeli to finance the Suez canal purchase.  They might
also have been models for the recent TV series  THE WAY WE LIVE
NOW !  Certainly the English nobility had problems with
accepting   them !

ASHDOWN HOUSE

A most unusual house and history is this property  in a
charming valley near to Lambourn, Newbury.  It has the look of
a square dolls' house, a 17th century Dutch style property
in downland  position, designed probably by William Winde for
Lord Craven.  Craven was a lifelong admirer of the sister of
the ill-fated Charles I - his sister being Elizabeth,
who married the ruler of Bohemia and had the name of the winter
queen.  It was her son Rupert who performed so brilliantly as
head of the Royalist cavalry in the 1640s.

Elizabeth never came to Ashdown but it did not stop Craven
dedicating it to her:  it is 3 storeys high with central cupola,
has enormous staircase rising the full 3 storeys, and is packed
with wonderful furnishings.  Opening is restricted and I have
never been able to get there at one of the few times it is
open, but it is a glorious spot from the outyside.

BASILDON PARK, NEAR READING

A mansion on the grand palladian scale, built in the 1770s and
1780s by the famous John Carr of York for Francis Sykes,
one of those Englishmen who went out to India and who made an
enormous fortune - and then came home to enjoy it by building
this impressive house.

## 36

The situation is 7 miles north west of Reading along the
A329, by the village of Lower Basildon and with fine views,
expanses of woodland and the Thames safely away to the north east.
Pangbourne and Goring are the neighbours. The house has
central pediment over great portico, with 3 floors and the
central one being the chief living area of grand rooms.
The ground floor roofline follows to the twin 2 storey
service quarters. Most impressive and rescued from decay in the
20th century by Lord and Lady Iliffe. The NT have spent
lavishly on it and the grounds.


BATEMAN'S

IN the Sussex countryside and downs near Burwash in the
Weald, and the home of Rudyard Kipling from 1902 until
his death in 1936. This is one of my favourites: a modest
small manor house type, actually Jacobean c1630 and built by
a local ironmaster grown prosperous in the decades after the
dissolution of the monasteries and spread of monastic wealth
to the other classes of society had encouraged thousands to
build thus. It is beautifully situated away from the mainish
road from Burwash, down tiny lanes and in an almost parkland
setting - the diminutive river Dudwell abuts, then there is
a fine formal lawn and garden, orchard and walled garden,
great favourites with the elderly in the sun.

One would expect a rabbit warren type of house; and thus it is.
Living rooms, study, bedrooms, hall, to an extent altered by
Kipling and his famously difficult wife and their assorted
servants and 3 children. His old Rolls Royce is mothballed
behind glass, and so many of his personal items remain on show
that you need hours to view and to read them. Strange
window in the hall where Mrs K could look down on the hall and
spy on the servants.

Kipling was one of my father's heroes, an Imperialist of the
first rank after a few years in India, much travelled,
world famous in his writings and now scarcely ever mentioned
anywhere in public beyond the Jungle Book cartoon !

How fashions change ! The house remains a star though -
plus excellent tea rooms with very creative and wholesome
food at lunchtimes. The only problem is that on the occasions
we have been we felt positively juvenile bearing in mind
everyone else at lunch was over 70 !

## 37

## BEMBRIDGE  WINDMILL

Set on the open land, downs almost, above Bembridge in the middle
of a field is this c1700 windmill with all its machinery and
equipment in tact, the only Isle of Wight survivor when once there
were dozens.   Do not get too excited: the views from the 2
tiny windows are good but everyone else wants to see too;
the car park is poor: there are no facilities; and it is
fairly dull viewing unless you are an addict of industrial
buildings !   Bottom of my list, and the 2 occasions we
visited with the children the elderly custodian was also
near the list bottom too ! Pity since it gets packed.  The scope
is obviously there - but you need to climb ladders.

## BOARSTALL DUCK DECOY

I recall seeing this most unusual 17th century duck decoy, in
working order, from the M40 one autumn afternoon: it is set
on the reed fringed lake and     looks so picturesque,
but was once an important means of catching the birds for the
winter table.  It is a few miles from Thame on the
Oxon/Bucks border - we have seen it from the road too but the
opening times are very restricted so better luck to anyone who
can time their visit to the district with the NT hours !

## BOARSTALL TOWER

JOhn de Handle built the only Buckinghamshire  medieval moated
fortified manor house in the earlier 14th century, and sadly the
lot was demolished in the 18th century.   The moat and earthworks
remain but the star in this setting near  Thame is the
great  gatehosue of the same date though altered in the 16th and
17th centuries and made into a house in the 1920s.
It is impressive and very hard to burgle one would imagine:
all stone, twin large hexagonal towers, arrow slits and
battlements,  bay windows and ballustrading,  and hood moulded
arched doorways.  Most interesting old gatehouse, then hunting
lodge and banqueting suite before being a home.

## 38

BODIAM CASTLE

On a million calendars and millions of cards and books is this
perfect 1380s castle: all that a child would imagine it to be
and more, but be warned that it is very popular and gets
packed with foreign schoolchildren !  It is to a French design
made popular in the early 13th century , adopted by Edward I
for his Welsh castles in the 1280s, and then built here both
for massive defence capacity and comfort.   It is thus outdated
for the time.  It was the response of  the Dalyngrydge family to
French destruction of the Cinque ports in the late 14th
century, a great perfect square with vast angLE  towers and
set in perfect moat on rising land with bridges on 2 sides
off the middle entrances.

The chief, north entrance has its great gatehouse mainly gone,
but the bridge and walk across is impressive, and  allows an
appreciation of its might.  However the surprise, and what
makes it distinct from its earlier Welsh and French counterparts,
is the creation of a large  4 range house with inner courtyard,
solely for comfort within the defences.  Much of course has
gone but you can explore and lose the children to an extent !

The setting is impressive but just grass, not much in the way of
trees - the calendars are deceptive on this point !  and
at the courtyard you can mix with a dozen nations.

The walk from the too small car park is quite a hike
uphill, so be warned; the toilets are too small for the coach
loads who come, but the cafe and facilities are quite good in
their timber buildings  with open garden and the river beyond.
A truly monumental castle but not at all typical and so far as
I know, never in battle.

BOX HILL

One of the best known beauty spots of the nation, and that rare
thing a hill in the district rising to 700 feet covered in
walks and paths, and once covered in box trees too.  It is
endowed with extensive views over the downland and the Mole valley
and  is not that far from Tadworth - much favoured by
Londoners.  Surprisingly busy but there is a lot to do including
centre, exhibition, cafe  and  Victorian fort.  Very nicely
presented too, but you do need  to be able to walk a lot to
get the most out of it.

## 39

## BRADENHAM VILLAGE

You park on the village green in this handsome village in
Buckinghamshire near High Wycombe, then walk round the
 grey flint church and red brick manor house plus the
cottages set nicely baout.  The church of St  Botolph is
an interesting mix from Saxon and Norman through to the
drastic restoration of the 19th century; the manor house
is 17th century, classical brick and decor with hipped roofline
and fenestration of that era.  It became famous as childhood
home to the illustrious Tory MP and  prime minister
Benjamin Disraeli, earl of Beaconsfield, whose father Isaac
D'Israeli lived in the manor from          1830 to his death in
1848.  Dizzy was educated at home, the family  regarding
the elite public schools and similar as appalling places.

Dizzy was a famous MP, member of the socalled Young England
group, author of many contemporary novels and articles, and
twice PM - his great rival being the Liberal Gladstone.
Amazingly Dizzy's novels were hugely popular in the 1840s but
have rarely been looked at since - I had trouble finding a copy
of any of them in the 1970s and he seems, like Kipling, to be
a neglected author.   As Queen Victoria said (and she far
preferred Dizzy to Gladstone), it is alleged, an evening spent
with  the former left you thinking you were the cleverest
woman in England; with the latter, you came away thinking he was
the cleverest man of the nation !

Dizzy settled down the road at Hughenden manor with his
much older wife.

## BRIGHSTONE SHOP AND MUSEUM

One of the pleasures of the Isle of Wight is this ancient village
with its largish Norman church and handsome old cottages and
farms plus hundreds of new properties overwhelming the
formerly much  spread out village.  Within the last 50 years
its population  has quadrupled though many are let homes.
The shops is a nice       little NT spot incorporating the free
museum chiefly dedicated to the lifeboat crews over
the eras.  It is wholly charming thatched and rough stone
vernacular, typical IOW, and on a desperately narrow lane which
is also characteristic of the isle: watch your head and     back,
traffic and low roofs !   Lovely view down the bottom of the
lane to the sea a mile or so away - villages needed to hide in
the trees and down like this one, from the ferocious wind of the
back of the Wight !

## 40

## BUCKINGHAM CHANTRY CHAPEL

On Market Hill in the centre of this fairly old world county town
of Buckingham is the small chantry chapel , in origin a Norman,
12th century chantry chapel where the priest prayed for the
soul of the founder.  It became the old Latin school, a sort of
classics school, after the Reformation when the thousands of
such chapels were dissolved, and the priests forced to earn
another living.  It is the oldest building of the district
and was rebuilT  during and after the medieval centuries,
finally receiving restoration from the famous Sir G G
Scott in the 1870s.  It is quite an object lesson in how
things used to look, and quite charming.  It was endowed as
a school in the 1550s by royal command and money.
Nice town centre is to hand and some pleasant walks along ther
river Ouse.

## BUSCOT OLD PARSONAGE

One of the NT properties which I have only seen from the
outside because tenanted and with seriously restricted
opening times.  It is on the banks of the river Thames in
Buscot near Faringdon, in either Oxon or Berks, depending on
your date.  Parsonage or rectory, old church, mansion and
village form a fine prospect.  The parsonage is a 1700s
Cotswold stone property and handsome, or a type familiar to all
those who have toured the district.

## BUSCOT PARK

The NT have a lot of land hereabouts and centring on this
c1780 neo classical house, packed with the best quality
furnishings and paintings.  E L Townsend designed the
house and though it was altered and extended in Victorian
times, these additions have been swept away and the whole ensemble
restored to its 1780 look.  Famous landscaped 18th century
gardens too, and  the  Italianate water garden is a feature of
the landscaping work in the 20th century by Harold Peto.
Fountains, cascades and statuary grace the whole, and you can
wander across the best part of 4000 acres of NT land.
Well worth a day out.

## 41

CHARTWELL

Situated close to the M25 in Kent2 miles south of Westerham is
this house, home to the illustrious Sir Winston Churchill
from the 1920s to his death 40 years later and much revered
by his admirers.  It is a strange house, home to a great man
but not a great house, and an odd mix of motifs and styles -
some 18th century , others from the serious rebuild  in 1923
for Churchill - who was permanently short of money and worried
about          financing everything.

The gardens are to an extent far more satisfactory, and
beautifully laid out and cared for especially on the terrace
and rose garden and water garden areas.  Interestingly there
was not much of a garden before the 20th century creations,
whereas the house has medieval roots.

The house is packed with interest if you admire Churchill and
his family - endless  associations with his long and
glittering public career and long life, though for me it was the
paintings of his which caught  my attention - that and the
great wall he spent some years building for a hobby !  One would
expect such things and his admirers will not be
disappointed !  Lovely walking country too, but note that it
does get busy  so near to London !

CHASTLETON HOUSE

I first visited this house some years ago when looking for the
church, and found it amidst the undulating Cotswold countryside
with its corn and other crops blowing on the windy but sunny
summer's day: it is a beautiful place to dwell, and isone  of the
best Jacobean properties of the nation.
A Witney wool merchant made money - Walter Jones - and in the
timehonoured way decided to buy a small estate and to build a
manor house thereon - which he did between 1602 and about 1612.

## 42

It is a manor house with 3 storeys and basement, plus that memorable row of 5 narrow gables plus large staircase towers: stepped gables and pinnacles, and projecting central bays, provide that extra impact. The ensemble is square and with a small courtyard, and though people sometimes think the famous Robert Smythson of Hardwick fame built it, there is no evidence.

Endless decoration inside of the most expensive type, and you will enjoy the furnishings. Outside is a notable stone gateway and stable block of the same Jacobean vintage and later dovecote. The layout of the gardens are typical of the same date and the NT are proud of the fact that it was here in the 1860s that the rules of the modern game of croquet were codified and formalised - so you can think on that as you play your next game!

These days it gets packed and there is a seriously limited number of visitors allowed in the house, and you are warned about this and about the brisk walk - which reminds me of the trek at Snowshill in the Cotswolds - from the car park to the house. You need to be fit to get round NT places ! Things have certainly changed since I first saw the property in the 1980s when I simply parked on the roadside grass. Lovely spot.

CLANDON PARK

This mansion is 3 miles out of the ferociously busy and wealthy county town of Guildford in Surrey, and is another local favourite which becomes awfully over populated. The original property was a gabled traditional Jacobean mansion which was entirely rebuilt out of all recognition for Thomas Onslow the owner, by Giacomo Leoni between 1713 and 1729. The result is described as the Palladian style mansion which has hardly been touched since. The NT are justifiably proud of it.

It is a rectangle of brick with stone dressings, beautifully fitted out inside with expensive collectors' items thanks to Mrs Gubbay in the 1920s and with gardens of the 18th century to cap it all off.

## 43

Clandon has a magnificent  2 storeyed marble house which marks it
off from most mansions,  the grandest of them all and quite
at variance with the rest of the rooms - modest if lovely
rooms.    Lord Onslow, governor of New Zealand in the 19th century,
brought back  a Maori house : not the everyday sort of thing in
Surrey !   And enjoy the Surrey regimental   museum too.


CLAREMONT LANDSCAPE GARDEN


On the edge of the town of Esher and some busy roads in Surrey
is this considerable garden venture - though the house is a
private school and not open to view.  The  famous soldier,
author and architect Sir John Vanbrugh built this house for
himself around 1709 and it was much extended by him when he
sold it to his friend the Duke of Newcastle, one of the
powerful Pelham family.  The lot was demolished c1770 by the
new owner Lord Clive and in came the duo of Capability Brown and
his partner Henry Holland.

However the garden  is of various dates: around 1715, then
by Brown in the 1770s,  and work by William Kent and others.
The NT are restoring the considerable area at vast   cost,
and there is a great deal to see including a  600 foot long
walled garden, lake and substantial garden buildings
and follies.


CLAYDON HOUSE


At Middle Claydon near Buckingham.  Ralph earl Verney built
a large mansion between the 1750s and 1780s, but this is only
a part of that building.  The exterior is deceptively normal and
plain, handsome but restrained: inside is a celebration of
 the extravagant rococco style, exuberant and unrestrained
opulence in every detail.  Be warned: you may well love it or hate
it !

## 44

Claydon had been an Elizabethan country house purchased by
the Verneys in 1620 and has remained with them ever since.
The whole was encased in red brick, given canted bays and
strapwork which is plaster to look like interlaced leather,
in Victorian times: it had been vastly enlarged in the 18th
century and one side was the best part of 260 feet wide,
but the owner invested badly and ruined himself, with the resultt
that probably over half of the massive new house was
demolished in the 1790s to save on maintenance.

Grand suite of rooms, splendid hall, endless carving and
decoration of the most fanciful sort, and one would not assume
such extravagance to be connected with the immortal Florence
Nightingale - the lady of the lamp. Florence, unmarried,
was appalled at the suffering of the ordinary soldiers in the
Crimean War of the early 1850s and hectored the government until
it allowed her to go out with volunteers to improve things.
The image one has of a kind and charming woman is deceptive -
she was notoriously aggressive, difficult and tough, and of
course she had to be ! She occupied rooms here because she
lived with her married sister Lady Verney for some years.

To an extent the southern England ideal of mansion, lovely
grounds and gardens, handsome nearby church and attractive
estate properteis and village - enjoy walking round its many bits
and pieces !

CLIVEDEN

I was outvoted when I said let us have afternoon tea !
Cliveden was restored in recent times and has become a very
expensive hotel, so you usually need to intend spending
money to get in. Interestingly you can moor your boat on the
Thames which forms part of the boundary, or simply go by car
to a vast car park , and the property is at Taplow near
Maidenhead in prime upmarket commuting territory. Everywhere
gets busy.

The original house was a 1660s country villa for the duke of
Buckingham on this incomparable site looking down the river
Thames - ie not across it, but as with Corby Castle for the Howards
on the river Eden in Cumbria and in a few other places.

## 45

Thomas Archer was brought in by the earl of Orkney to extend and
remodel in the early 1700s but it was largely burned down in one
of those regular country house fires, thistime  in 1745.
The flanking pavilions remained ok,  and these with the
splendid terraced, dictated  what would then eventually
happen in the rebuilds.  The famous country house builder and
architect William Burn created a new mansion in the 1820s
(after 80 years of dereliction) and linked the Archer pavilions
and terrace site.  This house too burned down in 1849, but
the owner was the enormously wealthy duke of Sutherland.
It was he who is famous for his Trentham palace and gardens
in  Staffordshire, and the great castle Dunrobin in
Scotland.   It was he also who drove a myriad of
highlanders off the estates for his sheep, and then built
coastal villages for them to develop new skills and ways of
life !   Which is of course why so much of northern Scotland
is bleak and empty of settlements, but the coast  has
large numbers of villages from this era.


The duke's wealth paid for the illustrious Charles Barry to
design a vast mansion which took only a year or so to built
build, such were the resources chucked at it: the new house
is described by the experts as an Italian villa on the grand
scale and in the Genoese style, a celebration of what money
could do with Italian or classical embellishment.

It reminded me of Clough Ellis's village in North Wales in
1 great block - Port Meirion that is.  Two and a half storeys
high, with ballustrading and decoration all over the place,
lavish  stonework and decor outside and inside the 1980s
creation of a hugh Edwardian style hotel - very effective but
presumably not as it was.

Marvellous interior design though it may not to be to the taste
of              everyone, and the formal gardens are a treat
with their stylised layout and planting.  All very Italian,
or Italian as it appears from time to time on the TV gardening
programmes !

The Astor family lived here for some years and odd programmes
on TV or newspaper articles note them, their home and the
legendary Nancy Astor.  Marvellous garden and grounds buildings
too including  work by Giacomo Leoni.

What I recall is the opluence of the interior, the wonderful
river and woodland views, and the grand terraced position of the
whole ensemble.

## 46

DEVIL'S PUNCHBOWL CAFE

A good deal of the once remote Surrey heathland and
woodland and common belongs to the NT, fortunately and
this cafe is close to the beauty spot famed for its
marvellous viewpoint and vistas across this and neighbouring
counties.  It gets extremely busy throughout the district so do
watch out, what with the A3 nearby and millions seemingly
passing every 24 hours .  Surrey into the later 19th century
was fairly remote and quiet, famed for its poor land and its
highwaymen at one time.    It remains a lovely county, the
lovelier it is the further you are from London and the
main roads.


DORNEYWOOD GARDEN


Set in the sylvan countryside round Burnham in Buckinghamshire
is Dorneywood, an 18th century house with Victorian additions
and chiefly remembered for its mural by Rex Whistler in the
1920s.  The then owner was Sir Courthauld  Thomson
who gave the house to the nation as a country retreat for a
cabinet minister in the 1940s (though nowhere  can I find it
telling me why he did this !).  It appears from time to time
on TV and in newspapers for hosting some international
person.

The house of course is private: the gardens will remain so to me
and most others since at the moment they are open by written
application only, and for appointments on 3 short afternoons
per year !

The gardens however, to the lucky few, are apparently a pleasure
to view.


EMMETTS GARDEN


A late 19th century garden specialising in trees and plants from
all over the world is to be found is the village of Ide Hill near
Sevenoaks in Kent.  Marvellous views all about, but again it  is
very popular indeed so go early or late in the day !

## 47

# GREAT COXWELL BARN

In a country setting, edge of Cotswold, is this enormous
13th century monastic barn complete with duck pond and goose
when we last went , and very few visitors.  It is stone with
slate roof and complex timber roofing: it measures 152 feet long
by 44 high  and about the same wide.  It seems to be
cross shaped, as befitted a barn of the great Cistercian house
at Beaulieu, Hampshire, and who gathered in the tithes here -
the 10 % tax on agricultural produce.  Lovely area and
building but little in the way of facilities on our last trip.
Enjoy the simplicity !  Tithes were largely commuted to tax cash
payment in the 19th century and then abandoned after rural
riots in the 1920s.   Faringdon is the nearest town.

# GREYS COURT

At Rotherfield Greys, near Henley on Thames on Oxon lies this
unusual property,  not far west of the town and in lovely
countryside.  The Grey family owned the site and the house on it
in the 1080s Domesday Book survey for the Norman king, and
the same family rebuilt in the 1340s to provide a defended
manor house of which much remains.  There is a keep of flint and
brick, 4 storeys, with 3 surviving defensive  towers,
part of the curtain wall, and then 17th century buildings added
by the  Knollys family who acqu red the property in Tudor times.
Much exists of the 17th century rebuild and extension - one
assumes that here as in so many places there was       not the
money to spend on demolition and total rebuild, with the
result that the house has grown almost         organically
over 900 years.  IN the 18th century the Stapleton family
remodelled the interior so that  it gives the impression of
an old country house with Georgian inside: the added on
bits and pieces and the outbuildings give the same charming
impression - not a house for the purists, but one to show off
how so many country houses have fared and ended up most
alluring !   Handsome gardens too.

## 48

HATCHLANDS PARK

Between East Clandon and  West Horsley in Surrey, not far from
Guildford, sits this mansion.   It is an important house:
built in 1756-57 for the illustrious Admiral Boscawen, it was
paid for with the proceeds of the captured French ships - it
being the custom for the seized prize ships to be bought by the
admiralty and the value split between captain, officers and
crew.  Readers may recall the numerous anecdotes about
sea captains growing wealthy on such prizes mentioned
throughout literature of the time, as in Jane Austen's
PERSUASION.

Even better than a hou    entirely of one style and a short
building span, is the fact that it was the first major
commission of the famous  Robert Adam, the young Scot recently
returnedfrom touring Europe and fresh from Italy in
particular.  It is often forgotten that he had a famous
father in the same field whose works cover Scotland, and
3 brothers too whose names are well known , and all 5 of the
Adam males did collaborate on and off and certainly
influenced each other.

It is assumed that Boscawen himself designed the vermillion
brick property in plainest Palladian and then invited Adam
to see to the interior: the result of course is most satisfactory
for visitors, though the Adam style is youthful and without
the lavishness, detailing and ornamentation of his later
work.

Of course various alterations took place in the next 200 years
including some building and         redecoration, but the whole
remains and suitably embellished by the last owner,
H S Goodhart-Rendel,    known for being an architect and
designer and who inherited the property in 1913.  He gave it to
the NT in 1946, and within the building is the   finest
and largest collection of     keyboard instruments in the world.
I first noted the property because of our own family
interest in strings, but here is a keyboard collection
connected with  Mahler, Elgar, Bach, Purcell, Chopin and
royalty   - do not miss it !

A few do not approve of the house because the interior is
by a young man as his first major commission fresh from 4
years abroad: but you will enjoy it and the Humphrey Repton
park setting, and that little gem of a garden designed by
the formidable Gertrude Jekyll - that       . elderly doyen of
gardeners everywhere who in so many commissions had the
illustrious young Lutyens as partner.  Happy days !

## 49

HINTON AMPNER GARDEN

In the Hampshire countryside near Alresford    and its own village
is this splendid 20th century and thus modern, garden, created
by Ralph Dutton, 8th and last Lord    Sherborne and usually
associated with the great estate of that name in the Cotswolds
between Burford and Northleach.  It is internationally
renowned as a garden and always worth a stroll.  The house
is however a different matter and being tenanted has a
seriously restricted opening time.  It was built in the 1930s
as a neo Georgian villa but suffered a grievous fire in
1960 and was rebuilt without the attic storey though with
some of the  historic items inside saved including old
plasterwork and woodwork from other properties which had been
brought here.

The most memorable thing after the garden and its scents and
colours is the collection of European furniture assembled by
Dutton .   Down the road is the partly Saxon parish church and
the district is one of ancient habitation.

HUGHENDEN MANOR

This mansion is at the head of the Hughenden Valley marked on
the maps which itself has been drastically encroached upon by
the expansion since the 1950s of that boom town of High
Wycombe,       furniture and  commuter capital of the district.
If you drive down the M40 towards the M25 you get panoramic
views across the undulating, hilly and wooded landscape of
some of the town and on to Beaconsfield though the house is
out of sight - it is a pleasant prospect for the motorist in
a fairly confined corridor through the Chilterns, and last time
I did it I noted an unusual bird of prey soaring above.  Days
later I found red kites had been released in the Chilterns and
to my great pleasure I  appeared to have seen one !  So keep a
look out !

The district is hilly and wooded and houses and villages
hide all over it.  Benjamin Disraeli was raised nearby at
Bradenham and bought Hughenden in 1847 when it was a

a part medieval manor house extended in the 18th century into
a large brick property.  Dizzy, leader of the Tory or
Conservative party (with Lord Stanley, later earl of Derby)
in the 1860s and PM in 1867 and 1874, called in an architect
of his acquaintance from London where he had lived during
parliamentary sessions - and presumably feeling the need for
a country house for extensive entertaining  (though he had
no children and his wife was much his elder) invited E B Lamb
to do something to the house.

Lamb first designed the  large monument to Dizzy's father -
to an extent a test for the house rebuild - and then turned
to the manor .  Lamb took     the stucco or protective
plaster on the outside and revealed the red and blue brick
under eath, added his own brickwork and Jacobean style
decoration.   The experts , feel it presents a plain Georgian
house with Victorian institutionalised feel, but it is
bold and dramatic and confident battlements and so on.   ONe
must admire it !

People like the interior which was         gothicisied in the
1840s and 1850s like so many such places,  and of course
the politician's life is everywhere in the detail and the
possessions strewn about: he made the Tory party
populist and successfully countered Gldstone and his
creation of a Liberal party out of the whigs.  Nonetheless his
obvious foreign origins, name  (which he changed from
D'Israeli),   Jewish inheritance and so on made him always
the outsider    the highest circles.

ONce he    had lost the election of 1880 and Gladstone had
announced he was retiring, Dizzy felt safe to go to the
HOuse of Lords as earl of Beaconsfield - he was always
popular with  Queen Victoria and got on famously with
her and Prince Albert, to the disgust of Gladstone.   Then
W E Gladstone  changed his mind (as he so often did) and came
   out of retirement to be PM on a number of occasions  the
Liberal Prime Minister.

Dwell in the grounds and garden, enjoy the woodland and
vistas.

## 51

## IGHTHAM MOTE

IN the deliciously wooded countryside between the A21
and  A228 lies this country property      described as the finest
medieval moated property of all, in a sunken valley and
dating from the 1330s. The manor house fits the environment
of woodland, undulating countryside and lake, and does not have
that dominating appearance one associates with such houses.
It fits its landscape nicely.

Much to see and to be enjoyed: entrance tower, some half timbering,
medieval stone windows and surrounds, great stack of medieval
chimneys in brick, hall, courtyard, almost a confusing array
of  rooms.  The great hall is the impressive point,but many
prefer the  14th century chapel, the undercroft, crypt,
Jacobean and 18th century decor and furnishings,
and much else - a complex but quietly satisfying
property.  The manor house of course enjoys its excellent
moat, though the name comes not from that but from the fact
that for centuries the local moot or meeting took place
here to run parish and rural and farming affairs.

The house also seems to be permanently being repaired and
restored, and indeed has been in this state for some years.
It was owned by various families and originally had a
substantial estate attached.


Famous walks and woodlands abound: the bridge across the
moat is a great focal point for tourists and you can see
a dreamy look on faces: but is it not damp to have a moat at
your house walls all year round ?  One wonders ...




## THE KING'S HEAD

In King's Head Passage , the Market Square in Aylesbury is this
ancient coaching inn, medieval and Tudor with later additions and
looking every bit the part of the sort of place used by travellers
for centuries.  It is of the courtyard type, timber framed and
packed tightly into the surrounding town centre spaces:

the town is attractive despite a vast office block for the
council, and here is the heart of the network of squares and
passages running in this ancient core.  It remains an inn
and you can enjoy hospitality for most of the day just as
old time folk did.  It retains some medieval stained glass-
in itself rare - and links with those county parvenus and
ultra rich folk the Rothschilds.

KNOLE

A precious survival in the expansion of Sevenoaks in Kent is
Knole, one of the largest mansions in Europe and literally against
the town's centre with its own parkland and some extensive
woodland despite the  scything effect of the main roads and
railways.  The house was originally a medieval and older manor
house in a fairly remote rural setting until the archbishop of
Canterbury bought it in the 1450s: Thomas Bourchier wanted a
large property to interrupt his journeys between London and
royal palaces, and his palace at Canterbury.  He then spent
lavishly on the place to create essentially the house of
today, which was ready during the 1460s.

Bourchier's successors as medieval and Tudor archbishops -
Morton and Wraham - also spent lavishly on this huge mansion,
and Henry VIII acquired the manor off their successor
Cranmer (later of the reformed C of E).

Elizabeth leased the property to one of her favourites,
Sir Thomas Sackville, partly to get rid of the enormous costs
of running it, partly to obtain the rent, and partly to
be able to have yet another noble house in which to stay for
a few weeks each year !

Sackville became earl of  Dorset in 1604 and bought the
property outright, and then commenced an extensive
modernisation project on a fabric already 150 years old.

Some battlements ,     low _ central tower, overall a feeling
that here is a huge late medieval palace built for comfort and
not defence, and with the enormous rebuilding to give it a
Jacobean flavour - all Jacobean gabling and windows, comfort and
decoration.

## 53

In the 18th century a large lantern tower was removed  from
one venue to the rear of the house and another tower, and
the several towers remaining are an interesting blend of
medieval with Jacobean and 18th century.    It is all an
odd but handsome composition and vast - I really can never get
over how extensive the whole ensemble is.

The house has 7 courtyards, 52 staircases or stairways,
and a staggering 365 rooms - though it is not entirely clear
is this is strictly accurate, but who cares !   And be advised
that a tour is not to be undertaken by the unfit or those who are
not keen !  It is  an exhausting business.

Vast amounts of furniture, paintings and so on to view, and
vast state rooms: great hall, kitchen, bedrooms, ballroom,
chapel and so on.   Extensive grounds and gardens too, and so
much to enjoy !

The cost of it all to the Sackvilles presumably prevented their
demolishing it - they had simply spent too much !


LAMB HOUSE


I recently spent some time in Rye, formerly on the Sussex
coast but now well inland, a Cinque port in medieval days and
tourist and residential honeypot these days: it is a handsome
place on a hilly site, all brick 17th to early 19th century, and
with little parking !  This house is typical, brick  and early
18th century on the corner of West Street in the centre, and
home to the famous writer  Henry James who occupied it from
1898 to 1916.  After him  came E F Benson whose series of
books based on   2 vying  grandes dames of town society-
Mapp and Luccia - enthralled 1930s society and were based on
his experiences in Rye.

The garden is perhaps  the star too, walled and colourful in
season, surprisingly quiet for so central a location:  the
house is packed with interest and of possessions of James,
whose works are now period pieces occasionally displayed on
TV in glamorous costumes - the BUCCANEERS  for example .
Benson's  MAPP AND LUCCIA  too had recent success in the 1980s
and certainly drew me to his home  (the town starred as

set for the series.


## LEITH HILL


One of the most popular open tracts of Surrey land and the
highest point of the south east: the tower  is an 18th century
Gothic folly and reaches to make the viewpoint 1000 feet above
sea level.   Richard Hill of the local mansion Leith HIll Place
built it in 1766 and kitted it out for occupation on a daily
fun basis but it all decayed eventually and  it is now restored.
It was described in one book as a remarkably accurate copy of
a Wealden tower of the middle ages.

The hill and surrounding area is fairly wild and open, but
you do need to be fit to get up the hills and to get to the
tower so be warned and wear good shoes and appropriate clothing !
The car park is not overlarge and you find the alleged 900
yard walk to the tower seems like 9000 yards.  Marvellous
views.


## LONG CRENDON COURTHOUSE


IN  a large and historic village in Buckinghamshire is this
unusual structure, stone on the ground and bla first floor
jettied or overhanging timber, terribly picturesque and only
open on the first floor.  This is one large room and a small
one, 15th century and used for the  meetings of the manor court
which oversaw the medieval doings of the manor.   They tended  to
die out in the 19th century but surviving buildings are quite
common, though not of this   quality.

The original purpose may have included parochial work -
accommodation for the clergy or some of them, together with
housing the vagrants temporarily or the local poor permanently
in the middle ages and later.  It also seems to have been used
for storing wool at one time and there may have been other
uses.  Interestingly the village is awash with medieval
properties so enjoy a walk round.

## 55

MONK'S HOUSE

An unusual property and one that has seriously restricted
opening times which prevented     our viewing is this
weather boarded  house in the village of Rodmell near
Lewes in Sussex, not especially attractive in itself but forever
associated with the writer Virginia Woolf and her
husband Leonard: she commite ' suicide, he died in 1969, and
recently a tenant was put in to look after the place.
Admirers of the Woolfs will see her possessions on view and
enjoy the links with the London Bloomsbury set between the
wars.

MOTTISFONT ABBEY, GARDEN, HOUSE AND ESTATE

Not long ago there were various programmes on the incomparable
trout river the Test in Hampshire, and occasional shots of this
place - Mottisfont village - appeared in idyllic surroundings
a few miles north of Romsey and Southampton.   The valley is
lovely and my father used to drool over the fishing, whilst he
had to make do with mostly northern streams and small but tough
fish.

The spot is named after a font or spring which continues to
send forth its water, and was a 12th century Augustinian priory
by the river Test which was converted into a mansion after the
1530s dissolution of all religious houses.  Lord Sandys obtained
the manor and converted the nave of the church into a
house, adding wings, long gone, and  then in the mid 18th
century a thorough renovation took place which added on to the
church to create the present property.

The house received a makeover in the Victorian era, and has
a notable  picture collection and the famous drawing room
art work of Rex  Whistler  and dating from the 1930s.
However the house looks Georgian in the main and has the
nave , of its medieval church  and parts of the west range  of
the cloisters, cellar and other parts from the dissolved house
built into it and exposed at various points.

## 56

My children always thought that such places such be left as
churches and as ruins, and that a place like this is spooky and
haunted: but it is charming, the gardens and park are
inspiring and the Test is a perennial pleasure - like the village
itself, and all owned by the trust  .

## MOTTISTONE MANOR GARDEN

Ample IOW car park on the downs looking south out to the
Channel, over the Isle of Wight's Back, and nestling in the
shelter of the Mottistone downland and extensive woodland lies
this ancient manor house.   The garden is on the sloping land
away from the house and open as per NT usual hours, but the house
opens 1 day a year and I have never yet made it !

The house is on probably a medieval or Norman and earlier
site, a substantial 2 storey house with dormers and L shaped,
but a puzzle to me: it certainly has 1560s work, but it has that
feel of a medieval  property so you can make your mind up
after you see the outside - arguably a 15th and 16th century
rebuild, made more harmonious in the 1920s by the owners who
were architects, and incorporating older work ?

The Cheke family owned it and built here, prominent in the 16th
century and one of their number marrying the illustrious
William Cecil, chief secretary to Elizabeth for 40 years.

The garden is quite a climb, all grassy slopes, some veggies and
fruit and flowers, wood fringed with badger gate - what damage
they do !  and fine barn in use for showing things off and
hiding the staff.   I first came here in the summer of 1960
to view the treat of the gardens: in the grounds today is
a shed for tea, and the jolly caravan type shelter with
all that 2 gentlemen needed for recuperating from their
architectural practice  in central London.   Seely, later Baron
Mottistone, was architect surveyor with his partner Paget to
St Paul's for many years, and his caravan shows off his
self contained existence if he so chose - including bunks,
stove, cupboards and so on.     His father had been a
knight and gentleman, a general involved in Canadian forces
and of fame in the 1914 war.  My father was much impressed and
recalled the stories about Jack Seeley.

Lovely place, with the IOW's only megalith , 13 feet high,
4000 years old, behind the house.   Get there on August bank
holiday !

## 57

THE NEEDLES OLD BATTERY


Park at the Needles pleasure park and pay £4 for the
privilege, and savour a 30 minute walk chiefly up hill along
the coast to this old fort, watching your step hundreds of feet
above the coasta and with the multi coloured Isle of Wight
beaches of Alum Bay and its surrounding area.  IN cool sunshine
it is perfect, watching out only for the occasional car and bus.

Interestingly this is one of a numerous forts on the island
built against the French and other potential invaders with the
result that Wight is studied with them - mostly small and
decommissioned long ago.  This one was an artillery fort
c1860, born of        continuing anxiety about the French even
though the Crimean War of the 1850s was fought alongside them
against the Russians - with the British generals, largely
schooled under Wellington and against the French, kept
referring confusingly to the enemy  as the French !  Readers will
doubtless know of the problems of this war !

Old Battery remains with its brick outbuildings, laboratory for
concocting the necessary chemical requirements of explosives,
changing rooms, cafe up what was the lookout post, and
parade ground with thick defences but most of the living
quarters simply gone.  Climb down the brick lined tunnel and
walk to see the observation point for searchlights against
shipping trying to sneak in, and enjoy the spectacular views of
the chalk Needles, the coast of the mainland, Hurst castle
almost coming across from there and more.

Once in thick fog we explored round, then ate upstairs to
watch the fog lift and revealing lost boats on a hot sunny
April morning.  All very English, and ensure the children have
been fed !


NYMANS GARDENS

Gloriously situated garden and house in the Sussex Weald, close
to suburban expansion but shielded mercifully in its charming
village and  setting from fast roads - but it does get busy even
in the wekdays.  Basically it is a large garden, sheltered,
with plenty of space, surrounding fields, vistas and woodland,
and with the house of the 1920s, half burned down, and looking
just like a medieval manor house intentionally.  Fine tea
rooms and facilities, big car park, and lots to see.

## 58

Why the wealthy Messel family should want a medieval manor house
on a ridge of land lying between 2 valleys, place a long
protected garden to one side, provide distant vistas, and
landscape the district I do not know, but it provides a fine
spot in the sun.  The house remaining is furnished and
equipped, and has endearing parts to it - the  Irish connection,
with Lady Rosse's chair and place where she opened the
champagne bottles, hitting the ceiling each time for years and
sending a spume of gas and champagne leaving a distinctive
trail: how the guides like to point this out !  As it is, it
would make a handsome house despite being ruined half or so.

We first took the wrong turn and could see the house slightly
above and beyond, so it meant a detour - and the early
information and blurb suggests this is just a garden.   Best
time to view ?   in the sun of early spring when all the
blossom is out without the leaves.

People will have seen a substantial old house for sale
in COUNTRY LIFE and other places, it being on the estate but
privately owned by Anthony Armstrong Jones as was, AKA Lord
Linley, whose family this was and which place  he recently
wrote about before being obliged to sell an underused asset
(he said).

Beautiful place indeed.


OAKHURST GARDEN

 Close to Godalming is Hambledon village, off the A283 and
cloe near to Chiddingfold and other spots of interest.  The
settlement is nicely surrounded by the undulating landscape and
its woodland, and is dotted with medieval to 18th century
minor properties.  One of them is the  small 16th century
Oakhurst garden, a timber framed cottage described as home to
a labourer of that era.   It is handsome and kitted out as it
might once have been: lovely garden, though it has to be said
that a poor labourer would have gone for food and herbs
rather than beauty and flowers.

## 59

OLD SOAR MANOR

In the heavily wooded countryside between Maidstone and Sevenoaks
is Old Soar Manor, Kent,  the solar or living end of a 13th
century manor house  dating from about 1290 and  with an
18th century red brick house standing by it where the great hall
and business end would have been.  The old manor is the NT bit,
2 storey with exhibition,  stone and with small chapel and all
those medieval bits and pieces one would expect in the way of
timberwork and masonry and decoration.  Smallish and not
too exciting, but homely and typical of a prosperous county
like this for the time.

OLD TOWN HALL, NEWTOWN

ON the Solent side of the Isle of Wight, miles from anywhere,
with the flat grassy and marshy landscape of the district all
about : there is no town, just a mid 13th century new town
foundation by the  bishop of Winchester who saw a chance to
improve his income, but it was destroyed in the French attacks of
1377.  What remains is a large nature reserve, scattered farms
and cottages, and not many tourist - so it is worth a visit
along the narrow lanes to reach it.

THe socalled borough remained such until the Reform act of 1832
got rid of most such places where there were a handful of
electors returning 2 MPs to parliament: the town hall was
the election place, and is 2 storeyed with ground floor,
modest entrance, nice main room, looking very Georgian.
The hall is brick with hipped roof and shows off an
interesting if modest exhibition of documents and pictures.
Ferguson's Gang , described inside, was a group of between
the wars secret benefactors to the NT as noted here.

The town hall is by itself : the 14th century roadway  and
houses have been mapped out, but this is a remote spot:
the huge watery nature reserve has some bizaarre  raised wooden
walkways, and you can see things like North African Egrets
wading around.

## 60

PETWORTH HOUSE AND PARK

The town of Petworth in Sussex might best be approached from the
A285 via Chichester, a winding, nicely quiet ,   wooded, steep
and charming run which suddenly throws up one of the most
handsome and least spoiled towns of the nation - oddly enough
in such a  region.  The road zig zags through the little town
and you pass, unwittingly, the outbuildings to the great house
where they cough pedestrians out into the centre and away from
the house.  Go further, think you have got lost, and find the
car park on your left going north and a long walk from the
property.  Be advised !

The last time we were there this enormous late 17th century
built by the duke of Somerset, with 2000 acres of park, great
lake and mass of deer , the famed woodwork and carving by
the illustrious Grinling Gibbons was being restored at vast
cost and inconvenience, but you could still enjoy the NT's
best collection of art both in pictures and in sculptures -
even my wife, not predisposed to enthusiasm, was keen to see
it !

You meet the mansion end on from the car park, then enter a yard
with the house on the right and the  enormous stable block on
the left, holding tea rooms, shop, and much more plus the
descending  huge covered passageway into the town centre.
The house was built by the duke after he married the last
Percy heiress - the Percy dukes of Northumberland being
amongst the premier nobility of the nation for      four
hundred  years until the male line failed in the later 17th
century and their properties were dispersed.

The Percy power base was Northumberland and Durham, but they had
manors all over, and Petworth had its medieval manor house
which the Percys turned into a castle in  c1310. A fair bit of
it remains within the mansion, strangely enough, in the
chapel, hall undercroft,  and so on.

The 6th duke of Somerset built the new mansion in the period
between 1688 and 1696, providing a magnificent show of power
in a west front of 320 feet length, but leaving most of the rest
plain and simple.

It had a dome and a great entrance, both now gone: the architect
is unknown but clearly there was one, and people always think of
French names.  The splendid west lost its entrance which was
moved to the back in the 19th century: the other main
front and the 2 sides are plain and described by many as
thrown together any old fashion !

## 61

The interior is a strange one from the point of view of mixed messages, grand and palatial, but evidently seriously interfered with by Salvin the great castle restorer of the 19th century: you therefore recall the great staircase and hall for size, not beauty; the state rooms for woodwork and marble and art and so on, not beauty; and wonder at the Turner paintings rather than at the splendour of the bedrooms. In the earlier 19th century at the end of the Georgian and into the early Victorian eras, the duke became pally with the illustrious painter Turner. The latter was middleaged and regarded as uncouth and strange, something of a loner but with a wonderful gift, and the duke employed him a good deal to preserve the beauty of the estate in his pictures.

Turner, son of a barber and closely involved with working on his only interest, art, cut an odd figure at the high calibre events hosted by the duke, but his work was without doubt a star event.

Enjoy the extensive grounds , lake and woodland, all depicted by J M Turner for his patron. You can go out down the passageway to the town then come back the same way with yout ticket, savouring a prime antique centre with fairly traffic free back courtyards and market place, a jumble of old houses and all subservient to the great house.

PITSTONE WINDMILL

This windmill near Ivinghoe in Buckinghamshire is dated 1627 but on the site of a much earlier fabric. It has been rebuilt or restored at various times and has a circular brick base with weah weatherboarded chamber above and then 4 sails. The machinery is there but unless you like this sort of industrial archaeology it can leave you cold !
There used to be a huge cement works locally.

## 62

POLESDEN LACY

Magnificently situated on the North Downs is Polesden Lacy,
a relatively modern house made famous for being HQ for the
Edwardian hostess for society, the Honourable Mrs Ronald
Greville.  The first house was a medieval manor house,
knocked down and rebuilt in 1631 and purchased with the manor
by the  playwright Richard  Sheridan 150 years later.
The site was the great attraction with those wonderful views:
it was in turn  replaced by a regency villa of the 1820s,
and finally this was entirely remodelled in the 1900s to create
a definitive Edwardian property.

The result is a handsome balanced quadrangle of a house,
with cupola and internal courtyard,  and with interiors and
decor of varying periods.  All is comfort and class,
beauty and elegance, and of course it was visited by all the
society folk of the time including royalty.  The gardens are a
match for the house: the Queen Mother honeymooned here in some
style in 1923 after marrying the king, George VI.  A place of
memories !   The house is near Great Bookham and Dorking.

PRINCES RISBOROUGH    MANOR HOUSE

IN a town at a gap in the Chilterns where much traffic funnels
through is this manor house, one of those handsome Jacobean red
brick properties which you would like to view but which is usually
only appointment only, and you come here once a year !
It was one of a number of historic houses taken under the wing
of the Rothschilds who then       renovated or restored to
what they felt it should have been originally: it has had some
distinguished owners        including the court artist Sir Peter
Lely, and is set in the  church district of the small historic
town centre.

## 63

## PRIORY COTTAGES

This is 1 Mill Street, Steventon , 4 miles out of Abingdon now
in Oxfordshire.  When I first ventured this way it was the
downs of Berkshire but the historic counties have had a lot to
put up with !   The Thames is not far off across the
busy arterial A34, with Oxford and Wantage nearby.  Didcot is
virtually over the road but the village retains its appeal.
These 2 cottages are part of the medieval ensemble of the
priory      that existed hereabouts: the most unusual causeway
put up by the monks is here too, to keep travellers and locals
out of the damp.  The priory was a socalled alien one , small and
owned by a French Order, and thus suppressed in the 1400s as part
of hostilities - and the money was useful to the crown too !
The great hall of the priory is incorporated in South Cottage,
and the Causeway is another medieval building, this time
timber framed.   Interesting what secrets lie beneath !

## QUEBEC HOUSE

In Westerham, Kent and close to open countryside and the
Kent coalfields is this red brick 17th century house famous for
being the home to General James Wolfe - the soldier long
forgotten by children these days, but to children of certain
generations as much a hero as Nelson and Wellington.  It was he
who became a general by ability alone - at a time when
wealth and connections meant everything - and who died at the
moment of victory when the British defeated the French in the
final battle for control of Canada  in 1759.

The house is an attractive one, square and with  gables all
about its 3 storeys, and a rebuilt earlier house probably of
the 16th century to judge by its fireplaces and so on - the
whole in and out was rebuilt.  Nice collection of Wolfe
material and the general has other places associated with him
    including nearby  Squerries Court and his mother's house
in Bath.   Wolfe was raised in the Westerham property before
joining the army young, and dying young too.

## 64

RIVER WEY AND GODALMING NAVIGATIONS AND DAPDUNE WHARF

One of the pleasures of the NT is its variety of properties and
this is a case in point: the river Wey looks harmless enough, tamed
even for centuries though parts are deep and dangerous, but
here in Surrey  it was the subject of extensive and early
improvement by landowners and business  interests seeking
a smoother and more accurate system for transport than that
allowed by the roads of the time.  It was improved, deepened and
more, in the 1650s and opened to barge traffic pulled by horses
in 1653.  The navigable Wey then went 15 miles and more
from Guildford where it linkled up with the navigable
Thames and onwards to London and the open sea.

Travel and transportation for goods was never the same thereafter.
IN 1764 a further 4 miles was made navigable to Godalming
above Guildford, bringing the benefits to a greater hinterland.
The NT have restored the wharf and you can take boat trips
along the navigations or hire all manner of craft in
Guildford and there is an exhibition and a lot to enjoy .
It is a novel and charming way to enjoy the river and
GUildford itself, though quite hard to find the riverside
  ocation strangely enough.  The site is behind the county
cricket ground for access, though it is easier by foot along
the ample towpath which you can walk all day.

RUNNYMEDE

In that strange district of the Thames meadows near Egham in
Surrey, packed with busy roads, industry and all that modernity
has brought to the far south east of England, is this spot,
greatly improved in recent years with its woodland and walks,
and now an SSSI.  It was on the site of this memorial  -
measuring simply as a piece of plain granite with inscription
relating to the signing of the Magna Carta here in 1215 when
King Johnn  acknowledge certain rights for his barons, with whom
he had been at war for years.  The actual signing may have been
in some other nearby spot of course in this marshy landscape
800 years ago !

The J F Kennedy memorial is nearby too, to the murdered
president, and various archaeological sites including that

of Norman St Mary's priory at Ankerwyke.  Plenty to see and do
and being near London, busy with Americans and other tourists.
The district was famed for its horse racing into the late 19th
century before the course was moved to the present Egham
track.

## ST JOHN'S JERUSALEM

This is a small property at Sutton at Hone,  just by the M25
and south of Dartford in what was Kent but is now commuter
London, with the Thames just to the north.  I have not been
able to get to this property but it is a chapel forming at one
time the east end of a Knights Hospitaller Commandery church
attached to what were the claustral buildings for living in and
which are now a private house.  The site is a fine garden with
the river Darent forming a moat: the rest of the church went long
ago and this is a precious survival.

## SANDHAM MEMORIAL CHAPEL

A strange and increasingly visited chapel of red brick,
built near Burghclere not far from the busy A34 near
Newbury.  The Behrend family commissioned it in the 1920s in
memory of relatives killed in the last war, but what makes it
remarkable is the series of 19 large pictures by the artist
Stanley Spence and executed by him in the 1920s for the
Behrends.  The scenes are those of the life of an
ordinary soldier in the 1914 war -  a lot of suffering is
entailed, and the 5 years of work by the artist are not to
everyone's taste !  Huge ressurection scene at the east end of
the chapel, and the inescapable message of suffering by the
soldiers.

## 66

SCOTNEY CASTLE GARDEN AND ESTATE

It is not especially prepossessing when you park after a long
minor road and  walk past the entrance and acess to the
rather interesting looking early Victorian mansion, partially
hidden, at the top of the hill: then you enter a steeply shelving
valley side with the enchanting ruin below in its protective
moat, and all is forgiven.

Scotney is a smallish ruined moated 14th century castle,
well hidden and not dominating at all, with a ruined 16th and
17th century mansion attached which looks as though you could
easily move into despite the damage.  The castle was put up
by the Ashburnhams as response to late 14th century attacks
on the district, and the  castle, towers and curtain walling
are on 2 islands .  Much remains to explore but you should be
able to enter the house rump - enchanting for children to
get inside such a place.

The Hussey family then brought in  Anthony Salvin in the
late 1830s for the large new mansion, and the hillside formed
part of the  quarry for the stone employed.  The new and
private house is Tudoresque and almost like a castle itself.
The gardens are beautiful, the views equally so, and access to
wide acres beckons those who are fit enough to take it all on.
Not much in the way of facilities so people tend not to
dwell long here, which is a pity.

SHALFORD MILL

On   the Guildford to Horsham road is this village of
Shalford,  pleasant but not special but rather improved by the
river Tillingbourne and the 18th century water mill on it -
a remaining example of Surrey domestic or vernacular
architecture, 3 storeys, tile hung and pretty, and a gift of the
Ferguson's Gang in the 1930s to the NT.  A projecting or
overhanging  piece adds to the charm though it was a strictly
utilitarian pieces  for lifting goods in and out upstairs without
the need to carry them inside and up stairs or ladders.

## 67

## SHEFFIELD PARK GARDENS

Deep in the Sussex countryside  between Lewes and East
Grinstead is this estate centred on  the great Gothic
Revival mansion itself - a creation of the 1780s for
J B Holroyd, earl of Sheffield, and designed by James
Wyatt, but of course not open to view.  One of my expert guides
says that the stunning landscaped gardens and parkland were laid
out by L ncelot Capability Brown, another that they were
designed by Humphrey Repton, so one has to take one's choice
with the caveat that both might have been there !  The spring
and autumn shows are especially famous and the garden adorns
the cover of millions of books and cards.  IN Edwardian times
the owner A G Soames expended a fortune on developing the
landscape, and the centre pieces is the sequence of the 4 great
lakes to produce  a marvellous shimmer  on surface of water as
backdrop.

Down the road is the famous  station for the bluebell line.
You need a lot of time to view the gardens, and we have never
managed to provide sufficient to see its glories; lucky are
they who live not far off.

## SISSINGHURST CASTLE GARDEN

In the village of the same name, near Cranbrook in Kent is this
world famous garden, created by the writer and society
figure Vita Sackville  West and her husband the diplomat and
diarist Sir Harold Nicholson - they of recent films and books !
in the 1930s when they rescued the almost ruined site and
restored  the glory.

Most of the castle is private: the large gardens are broken      up
into a series of small self contained thematic gardens
vaguely along the Elizabethan fashion, incorporating brilliant
species of plants and shrubs and not the ideal shape or format
for the vast troop of tourists who come !  Indeed it looks like
being worn away at time.  The house was a grand Elizabethan and
 medieval courtyard mansion of which part remains: the red
brick prospect tower of 16th century vintage is open, being
workrooms for the garden creators and packed with interest.
A gem of the NT but hard to keep perfect in the crush.

## 68

## SMALLHYTHE PLACE

Famous as home to the actress Ellen Terry from 1899 to
1928 and for its theatre and museum  is this 16th century
half timbered house in the village of the same name between
 Hythe and Tenterden in Kent.  Ellen's museum is devoted to her
own life and work and to earlier actors - Garrick and Sarah
Siddons over 100 years before for example - plus her own
associates like Henry Irving - an important place of
pilgrimage for those keen on the dramatic world.

The tiny village is on the river Rother and was in the middle
ages a port and shipbuilding centre, in work for royal craft it
into the 16th century - Smallhythe PLace and    other properties
in  similar style  were  built in late Tudor times at the end of
the port era .  I recall the theatre made out of a barn appearing
in a situation comedy in the early 1980s with George Cole as
star, and the theatre is usually open to view and still in
use.

## SOUTH FORELAND LIGHTHOUSE

This is simply a whitewashed looking lighthouse complex on the
ciffs at the considerably grown settlement of St Margaret's
at Cliffe , separated from Dover by  a splendid stretch of
coastline and cliffs: you need to be fit since we have to walk
for what seemed like an hour from the designated car park,
simply to get to the viewpoints and building which was not open
on that day.  The illustrious radio pioneer Marconi used it,
not surprisingly, in his ship to shore  radio communications
experiments in the 1900s.  It seems to be very windy too,
so lighter and frailer folk need weighting down !

## SPRIVERS GARDEN

A 1750s brick house surrounding a core of much earlier timber
framing property, in one sense country style Georgian for the
time, but with that interior history well beyond 1750.

## 69

The house never seems to be open; the handsome little garden is open 3 days per year.  Set in Horsmonden near Paddock Wood in Kent.


STANDEN


Down a lane and 2 miles or so out of East Grinstead in Sussex is this large country house, atthe end of a fairly long drive, past the various facilities, and a smallish car park beckons.  Round the corner - a shorter walk than is usual ! - is the house, and then to one side is the large and sloping garden site with distant views (though not especially wonderful).

The house is regarded as a family house showpiece of the Victorian arts and crafts movement, built in the early 1890s by Philp Webb, the architect par excellence of the movement which developed out of Burne Jones and Morris and their wide ranging circle.   I live near one of Webb's major buildings, the Brampton parish  church in Cumberland, and have often          admired his work, but I find Standen unsatisfactory merely  as an observer for it is a strangely mixed design, better in than out, though doubtless opinions vary.

Outside it is a medley of  building materials - different colour bricks, stone, tile hanging, pebbledash, weather boarding and so on so that more or less all materials of the region are shown off.  Then there are the enormously high chimney stacks, and Georgian windows with that distinctive segment heading. Lots of gables, a ferociously expensive design to execute and above all to repair (though labour was cheap in those days and no problems getting plumbers etc !).

The plan is described as informal, which means chaotic to some extent, and the whole has that distinctive tower - big and impressive but just odd !  Large stone entrance porch too, projecting right out to welcome you.

I prefer the interior: decorated throughout in William Morris carpets, wallpapers, fabrics and furniture, with sympathetic contemporary (to the 1890s ) paintings, tapestries and all else.  Large original fireplaces too, and approved of by my family.  Compare it with Wightwick near Wolverhampton.

Nice to have a family house on this scale though, and oozing such quality throughout !

## 70

## STONEACRE

In a district famous for its Kent timber framed period properties
is Otham, and here is  Stoneacre, a half timbered yeoman's house
with famed great hall dating from the 15th century.  It is
described by some as a Wealden house, and has wings added
possibly in the 16th century with gables.  It was added to
from another property thanks to work by Aymer Vallance in the
1920s who restored and enlarged what was already  a
handsome property, and now in a suitably    cottagey garden.
All very pretty and surprisingly busy at times.

## STOWE LANDSCAPED GARDEN

3 miles out of Buckingham is this magnificent mansion and its
counterpart gardens, though the house is a private school  and
not open to public view.  The mansion was 16th century and owned
by the  Temple family when it was rebuilt in the 1670s
and rebuilt again in the 1770s by Adam into one of the major
mansions of the nation - quite formidable and huge.

However the landscaped garden is the important bit for it was
here in the 1730s that William Kent, inspired by the poet Pope
and his own travels in Italy, who created  a naturalistic
style of gardening in what was regarded as harmony with
Nature.   It was the first ofthe the socalled English
landscapes, and  the head gardener, Lancelot Brown, in the 1740s
further developed the capabilites of the site and style and
earned his nickname.

After 18th century spending on a vast scale, the family
had financial problems in the Victorian era and sold up in the
1920s, with the house and grounds saved by the school from
destruction.  The NT took the  gardens c1990 and work in
restoring and improving has gone ever since.

The huge grounds or garden have more than 30 historic and
surprisingly grand buildings dating from the  18th and eaerly
19th centuries - temples, arches, monuments, tower, castle and
more.  It is these  that you recall with the lakes and
the vistas of trees .

## 71

Whilst the garden is one of the great NT attractions, it is also
an enormous source of expenditure in restiring the buildings
and replanting on a collossal scale: it remains one of the wonders
of the

## UPPARK

I recall the great fire of 1989 when builders who had just spent
millions restoring this house near  Harting in the Sussex downs
left a blow torch on when they went for lunch and burned down
the lot !  A famous court battle      ensued and the builders
eventually lost , and the whole was then again rebuilt for
millions.  The exhibition block shows off the dramatic fire
video, and there are extensive grounds to enjoy before a hike to
the house itself.

Uppark, distinguishing it from Downpark, is literally atop of a
hill, with magnificent   seaward   and downward views,
and hidden from access points so that the whole comes as a
surprise to the tourist.  It is a sort of giant dolls house,
in brick and stone,  simple and elegantly proportioned,
something of a Dutch style imported here  and made elegantly
basic but handsome - described as masculine by the experts !
Richly ornamented modilions or brackets under the great eaves,
but plain stone and brick throughout.

It was built to designs by an unknown architect about 1690
for Ford, lord Grey of Werke and later earl of Tankerville.
The Fetherstonhaughs came into possession in the 1740s
from the Northumberland and Cumberland family.  They made the
house decor what it is today, fine and notable 18th century
work.

Fine set of  main rooms on the 2 floors plus attic storey
but the surprise is the service corridor, largely underground
but with some windows, linking the house to the service block -
today quite an adventure for everyone.  In Victorian
times H G Wells the novelist was raised here since his
mother was housekeeper - an interesting connection.
Shades of illustrious architects and designers throughout the
building and especially work of Humphrey Repton: interestingly
William Talman, famous early architect, is suggested as the
             designer of 1690.

## 72

THE VYNE


At Sherborne St John in the countryside near Basingstoke in
Hampshire is this notable Tudor property, originally built
by Lord Sandys, lord chamberlain to Henry VIII, and
receiving 17th century classical rebuild over part of its fabric.
The latter work was by the Chute family of parliamentarians and
lawyers; then in the 1760s John Chute, a pal of the famous
arbiter of taste and fashion Horace Walpole, renovated and
embellished, and again in the mid 18th century the final
touches happened to the mansion.

The whole is rose coloured brick, patterned with diamond
diapering but gently, and a replacement for the older medieval
manor house of which nothing recognisable survives in its Tudor
rebuild. It was far larger than the older or newer versions,
and for the time was considered very advanced - no moat or
rising great hall to the roof, huge windows and so on.
Internal arrangements were for comfort and have remained
mainly unaltered, though there was a serious problem for
sanitation alone which was remedied.

Chute removed the courtyards, replaced mullioned windows with
stone rectangular frames, and boldly commissioned JOhn Webb,
chief follower of Inigo Jones (by then dead) to put in the
great classical portico.

John Chute who altered the house in the 1760s had spent over
30 years in Italy and unexpectedly inherited the estate when
all of his brothers died childless. As second only to Walpole
in the Strawberry HIll gothic ideal, Chute
was remarkably restrained at the Vyne and his major work
was simply the great staircase and renovating the general
decor. The Victorians added battlements as an after
thought.

Beautiful furniture and furnishings - most folk like Georgian
and Strawberry HIll style - and fine grounds to explore.
Oddly and interestingly the building which sticks out
uncomfortably at one end is the large private chapel,
medieval into Tudor, with that rare thing a polygonal
apse of an east end -once common, later very rare.

The grounds have notable items such as the garden
pavilion and lodges to enjoy, though the house is always the
star.

## 73

WADDESDON MANOR

At Waddesdon near At Aylesbury in Buckinghamshire is this
wonderful Victorian creation of Baron Ferdinand de Rothschild,
in a famous village and countrys setting.  The new owner of
the estate had no house to burden his ideals, and simply
brought in an army of workmen who levelled a hill to create
a flat site for the mansion and room for the extensive
grounds, garden and parkland.  It was specifically for the
huge house parties of this enormously rich and society-
leading family, and today its          restoration has meant
it is a huge draw  to tourists and caters for their needs.

Readers who have seen the great late medieval chateaux of
Chambord or Blois in the Loire valley of France will be
familiar with the style of this mansion created mainly
between 1877 and 1883 for the Baron by his architect
Hippolyte Destailleur with 2 wings added by the architect's
son Andre in the 1880s.  It is of finest Bath stone, 2 high
storeys but with grand dormers and a wealth of French
renaissance decoration,  huge porte cochere, wings like vast
pavilions,  domed towers, spiral staircases, high chimneys and
enormous width.  All built to stun and to impress.

The interiors are remarkable too, especially for their lack of
medieval renaissance decor except in 1 or 2 rooms, for the
house is chiefly an interior of bought interiors from French
hotels and buildings of the  18th century - a riot of
fine art, furnishings and the like from   older French sources,
and quite spectacular.  A slow troop through the rooms is
simply not enough to appreciate their brilliance !

A wonderful garden too, especially for its colour, its
outbuildings and garden buildings, stables and above all the
fabulous  iron and metalwork aviary - built at enormous
expense to copy the one of the Baron's childhood home near
Frankfurt.  It has just been restored to its 1880s
splendour and is a stunning embellishment to the formal
garden with its exotic species inside.

Ironically the considerable estate village was built to
service the huge estate, but its style is late Victorian half
timbering arts and crafts movement ! a Nice contrast indeed for
the Baron   lavish French creation !

Wonderful place to spend the day.

## 74

WAKEHURST PLACE


One of the major attractions of the NT is this house and garden
at Ardingly near Hayward's Heath in Sussex  and these days with
a substantial Kew Gardens presence as one of their research
facilities.   It is in fact administered by the Royal
Botanic   Gardens.   The countryside is handsome and inviting and
the Loder Valley nature reserve is adjacent to this huge site.
I doubt most people ever see most of it simply because of its
sheer extent,  and though the research facility is  closed off
to the public there is an extensive visitor's centre, largely of
glass, all high tech and ultra modern and impressive for the
children.

The Culpeper family built a courtyard house in the Elizabethan
era, probably  around 1590, and this had its back half and
courtyard demolished in 2 rebuilding phases of the 17th century
and the 1840s to create the present E shaped property, still
impressive and with those tea rooms behind.  Inside the
house  is a welcoming exhibition about the estate and the work of
Kew et al, so do not expect an  historic interior despite the
Elizabethan classical exterior and such furnishings as fine
staircase and chimney pieces.   It is all about
the plant world.

Huge gardens, arboretum, lawns and parkland, endless drives and
so on so make sure you are fit !    I always think such places
need animals or birds on show somewhere to add to the
panorama of plant life from round the world.




WEST GREEN HOUSE GARDEN


In Hampshire, a mile out of the High Street of the village of
Hartley Wintney, lies  West Green with its  18th century
     country house - West Green House, occupied and never open,
but in an NT garden.  It is a handsome country Georgian property
with Queen Anne origins and perhaps earlier hidden behind  the
plaster work, but it is the garden which is open to be
enjoyed.   A tranquil spot to be.

## 75

WEST WYCOMBE PARK


One of the most famous or infamous houses and estates of the NT
lies  at West Wycombe in Buckinghamshire close to
High Wycombe and the A40.  The lot was created by the
prominent MP and libertine Sir Francis Dashwood in the mid
18th century with the facades of the mansion looking exactly
like  classical temples on top of each other.  It is a
staggering design.

Dashwood lived from 1708 to 1781 and held various government
posts after having spent some time touring most of Europe.
He formed a private male club - quite usual in those times -
and like many others it had its official name (the Knights of St
Francis of Wycombe) but was also known as Dashwood's Apostles
(and with others, the Hell Fire club).  Much is made of the wild
revels of the clubs concerned !

Dashwood took the Queen Anne family house and drastically
altered and enlarged to create his classical temple on all sides
and both storeys, a fantastic visual        feast of
ornament and decoration which certainly staggered me.
Dashwood seems to have been the chief inspirer of the
design though he used several architects, mostly unknown, to
carry out his extensive plans in the 1750s.
The interior is  as one would expect, a celebration of all
that the 1750s thought a  classical suite of rooms should have
in the way of extravagant decor, and looks wonderful  - though
could one live with it day in day out ?

The grounds are likewise on the grand 18th century scale and
received various attentions from designers throughout the
18th century and including Humphrey Repton.  The river Wye
was dammed, a lake created, and the grounds liberally stocked
with classical  follies   et al.

There is a striking family mausoleum on the hilltop above the
wooded and landscaped hillside and valley, and an interesting
church.  In one hillside is a series of caves that are
open to view at a price, used by the Dashwoods for their
fun and games,  but you need to be fit to get round them and
walk all about a huge area.

THe village itself is  largely a creation of the Dashwoods.
Fascinating family and place !

## WEST WYCOMBE VILLAGE AND HILL

Mentioned earlier: remember London and the 12 million
people of the region live within an hour's travelling and
it gets busy all the time.  Lots to see and to enjoy including
handsome High Street.

## WHITE CLIFFS OF DOVER

Extensive chalk downland, visitor attractions and so on,
mark this famous spot in Kent: gateway to the nation from
Europe, famed in song and history, and well worth a journey
to view it.

## WINCHESTER CITY MILL

Situated at the foot of the High Street in the city of
Winchester is the historic  city mill on the river Itchen,
an ancient part of city business life and providing the
essential service of milling corn into flour.  It was entirely
rebuilt on  the historic site in the 1740s and has recently
been renovated and restored once more but I have not seen inside
since then.  It is very photogenic,  accessible to tourists,
and has a lovely island site and garden to be enjoyed.  It is
now a great attraction.

ILLUSTRATIONS

REFERENCE to

| | | |
|---|---|---|
| 1 | Alton . | 20 |
| 2 | Andover . | 21 |
| 3 | Barton Stacey . | 22 |
| 4 | Basingstoke . | 23 |
| 5 | Bermondspit . | 24 |
| 6 | Bishops Sutton . | 25 |
| 7 | Bishops Waltham . | 26 |
| 8 | Bosmere & Hayling . | 27 |
| 9 | Bountisborough . | 28 |
| 10 | Buddlesgate . | 29 |
| 11 | Christ Church . | 30 |
| 12 | Chutely . | 31 |
| 13 | Crondall . | 32 |
| 14 | East Meon . | 33 |
| 15 | Evingar . | 34 |
| 16 | Fareham . | 35 |
| 17 | Fawley . | 36 |
| 18 | Finch Dean . | 37 |
| 19 | Fordingbridge . | 38 |

The ISLE OF WIGHT is a County of itself.

London, Published by Henry Teesdale & Cº 302, Holborn.

Longitude West from Greenwich.

'Ring out the False: Ring in the True.'

# CHURCH BELLS

### EDITED BY J. ERSKINE CLARKE, M.A.

7.—*Vol. IV.*     *SATURDAY, December 27, 1873.*     *One Penny.*

THE CHURCH OF ST. MARY-LE-BOW, CHEAPSIDE.

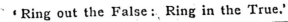

'Ring out the False: Ring in the True.'

# CHURCH BELLS

### EDITED BY J. ERSKINE CLARKE, M.A.

—*Vol. VI.*      *SATURDAY, July 1, 1876.*      *One Penny.*

ST. GEORGE-IN-THE-EAST, MIDDLESEX.

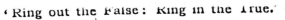
'Ring out the False: Ring in the True.'

# CHURCH BELLS

## EDITED BY J. ERSKINE CLARKE, M.A.

2.—*Vol. VII.*    [REGISTERED FOR    SATURDAY, *December* 1, 1877.    TRANSMISSION ABROAD.]    *One Penny.*

ST. LEONARD, SHOREDITCH, LONDON.

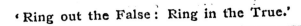

'Ring out the False: Ring in the True.'

# CHURCH BELLS

### EDITED BY J. ERSKINE CLARKE, M.A.

Vol. V.  SATURDAY, March 6, 1875.  One Penny.

ST. PANCRAS CHURCH.

'Ring out the False: Ring in the True.'

# CHURCH BELLS

## EDITED BY J. ERSKINE CLARKE, M.A.

J. VII. [REGISTERED FOR    SATURDAY, *January* 27, 1877.    TRANSMISSION ABROAD.]    One Penny.

ST. MATTHEW, BETHNAL GREEN, LONDON.

MATTHEW is the mother-church of the parish of Bethnal Green. appearance has probably become well known to most Londoners establishment of the Bethnal Green Museum in close proximity architecture is not such as to attract many visitors to it from intrinsic merits. It is said to be of the Doric order, and was built towards the middle of the last century, and consecrated in 1746. Though partially destroyed by fire in 1859, the walls were left standing, and it retains its original plan and unmistakable Georgian character. It is said that the frost at the date of the fire (December 18th) was so severe that the water froze as it was poured on the burning ruins. It was rebuilt by a rate on the parish and re-opened in 1861. The Rev. Septimus Hansard has been Rector since 1864.

# CHURCH BELLS

### EDITED BY J. ERSKINE CLARKE, M.A.

Vol. VIII.    [Registered for    SATURDAY, March 23, 1878.    Transmission Abroad.]    One Penny.

ST. DUNSTAN, STEPNEY.

the ancient churches in this country, few can compare in anti-
ity of origin with the parish church of Stepney. The present
the successor of one which was already standing in the time of
an. That great ecclesiastic rebuilt the original church, which
icated to All Saints. This took place, according to Matthew

Paris, in 952. But after the death and canonization of Dunstan the new
church was re-dedicated in his name, which it still bears. Not much
is known of the history of the church from Dunstan's time till the
reign of Henry VI.; though no doubt, like other churches, it had its
share of neglect, restoration, addition, alteration. About the reign of

Hawker

Frith

## THROUGH READING AND NEWBURY ON THE ROAD FOR BATH

Reading (lower photograph), though an old county town, has little elderly in its appearance.  There are, however, a few eighteenth century buildings in Friar Street, opposite the General Post Office.  Continuing on our route to Bath we reach Newbury, about seventeen miles from Reading.  Here there is an inn, the Jack of Newbury, named after a local hero, John Smallwood the clothier, who marched to Flodden Field in 1513 at the head of 130 men.  Our photograph shows the Broadway, with the Bath Road going off to the left.

113

Hawkes

**AN EXCURSION FROM THE MAIN ROAD: DONNINGTON CASTLE, HELD STOUTLY FOR KING CHARLES IN THE CIVIL WAR**

One mile from Newbury along the Oxford Road is a hill, seen to the left, which is topped by the ruin of Donnington Castle, which was built about the fourteenth century. It was held by the gallant Captain Boys in August, 1644, against the Roundheads. The assault was kept up for six hours and beaten off, the enemy losing 100 men. In September the castle was badly mauled by artillery, but still held out, and only surrendered in April, 1646, at the order of the king himself. Traces of the besiegers' earthworks are still to be seen, but the castle was destroyed by the Parliament. Further damage was done when material was taken from the ruins to build Castle House at the bottom of the hill

# BERKSHIRE.

EXPLANATION.

Market Towns with the Distance from London in measured Miles, as ...... }  WANTAGE 59¼

Churches and Chapels ............... +

Turnpike Roads. ========  Mail Coach Roads.

Bye Roads ...................

Navigable Canals ...................

Rivers ...................

Seats of the Nobility and Gentry ......... ▪

NB. The figures on the Turnpike Roads show the distance in measured Miles between the Towns.

Population 145,289. Assesd Taxes £51,449.

London to Reading
by Wokingham 39¼
    Binfield .....38¼
    Maidenhead 39
    Windsor ....40¼

Scale.
0 1 2 3 4 5 6 7 8 9 10 Miles

# SHIRE.

## EXPLANATION.

Market Towns with the Distance from
London in measured Miles, as ...... ⟩ **WANTAGE** 59¼

Churches and Chapels ................. +

Turnpike Roads. ~~~~~~ *Mail Coach Roads*

Bye Roads .........................

Navigable Canals ..................

Rivers ............................

Seats of the Nobility and Gentry ........ ◼

NB. The figures on the Turnpike Roads shew the
distance in measured Miles between the Towns.

Population 145,289. Asses.d Taxes £51,449.

BUCKINGHAM

GREAT MARLOW 31

Fawley

Cookham Dean

Cookham

Medmenham

Hurley

Pinkney's Green

Taplow

HENLEY upon Thames 35

Maidenhead Bridge

London to Windsor
by Datchet ...... 21
Slough ...... 22

MAIDENHEAD

London to Reading
by Wokingham 39¾
Binfield 38¾
Maidenhead 39
Windsor 40¼

Hampsden

Shiplake

Bray

Monkey I.d

Slough

Eton

Mapledurham

Caversham

Sonning

WINDSOR

Old Windsor

STAINES 16¼

READING 14

Woodley

Hurst

Warfield

Winkfield

Egham

WOKINGHAM or OAKINGHAM

East Hampstead

Bracknell

Ascot Heath

Virginia Water

Arborfield

East Hampstead

Sandhurst

Bagshot

Swallowfield

Finchampstead

Stratfield Say

Eversley

Blackwater

Yateley

Blackwater

SURREY

HANTS

THOMAS HOWARD, EARL OF ARUNDEL.

*(From the Portrait by Vandyck. In the Possession of the Duke of Sutherland. Engraved by C. Carter.)*

*HOWARD* Earl of *ARUNDEL.*

Til

Dixon-Scott

## THE LONG MAN OF WILMINGTON AND THE WESTBURY WHITE HORSE

The White Horse of Westbury (top) is probably better known than any other of his chalk species, since a good, if rather distant, view is to be had from the main Great Western Line to Taunton, via Newbury. It is supposed to commemorate Alfred's victory at Ethendune and measures 180 feet from head to tail. Its contours have been somewhat altered during the various "scourings" to keep the grass from blurring the chalk. The Long Man (bottom) is cut in the Downs behind Wilmington, between Lewes and Eastbourne, and is about 240 feet tall.

ishop Bethune (1131–48). In the first half of the thirteenth century the lady chapel was built and the north transept reconstructed. Bishop Herbert de Lozinga brought his throne from Thetford to Norwich in 1094, and two years later began building the present cathedral as the minster of a Benedictine priory. The fabric was completed by his successor, Eborade (1121–49). In 1272 the cathedral was pillaged by a mob, and in 1361 it was damaged by the fall of the spire, but repaired by Bishop Percy (1352–69). In 1463 and 1509 it was badly injured by fire.

Gloucester is another famous cathedral of the west of England, and really dates from 681, when a monastery was founded at Gloucester by Osric. This was replaced for a while by a college of secular canons, but finally reorganized as a house of Benedictines. In 1100 Abbot Serlo built a new minster for the monks. In the fourteenth century its choir was transformed into its present shape, and in the next century the lady chapel was added. In 1543 Gloucester was made a bishopric and its minster taken as the cathedral.

The first important religious institution at Oxford was the convent of S. Frideswide, founded in the eighth century. In 1002 its church was destroyed in the massacre of the Danes on S. Brice's day. It was rebuilt by Ethrelred, and at the Norman Conquest became the minster of a Benedictine priory. Prior Robert de Cricklade (1141–80) built for the monks a new church. In the next century a lady chapel was added. Cardinal Wolsey vaulted the choir, but in 1524 he dissolved the monastery and removed the greater part of the nave to build his new college of Christ Church. In 1541 the city was made a bishopric, and the bishop's throne placed in Osney Abbey, but in 1546 it was removed to Christ Church.

Two kings were concerned in the early beginnings of Peterborough and St. Albans cathedrals respectively. Peada, king of Mercia, founded a monastery at Peterborough in 659. It was destroyed by the Danes in 870, but was subsequently rebuilt by Bishop Aethelwold of Winchester. In 1071 it was again pillaged by the Danes, and was finally destroyed by a fire in the reign of Henry I.

IN 1117 Abbot John de Sais began a new minster, which was completed before the close of the century. At the end of the next century the West Front was erected, and in the last half of the fourteenth century the retro-choir was constructed. In the eighth century Offa, king of Mercia, founded a monastery on the supposed site of the tomb of S. Alban, who had been martyred by the Romans in 303. At the Norman Conquest the abbey was rebuilt by Abbot Paul de Caen (1077–93). His work was in part reconstructed by Abbots William de Trumpington (1214–35) and John de Hertford (1235–60). In the time of Abbot Hugh de Eversden (1308–26) a lady

Arnold

## BELL TOWER OF CHICHESTER DETACHED FROM THE CATHEDRAL

This is the only surviving cathedral belfry isolated from the main building. There used to be one at Salisbury, but this was demolished about 1789 by that ruthless "restorer" the architect Wyatt. The Chichester bell tower or campanile is 120 feet high, and commands a view which stretches south to Selsey Bill and the Channel. The tower was put up during the fifteenth century. Among the bells the oldest was cast in 1583, and on another, "Big Walter" weighing 74 cwt., the hours are sounded. The left-hand photograph shows the entrance.

King

**CHICHESTER'S SOARING SPIRE, A LANDMARK FOR SHIPS IN THE CHANNEL**

Chichester became the seat of a bishop in 1082, and Bishop Ralph de Luffa began building nine years later. In 1186 the building was again burned, and Bishop Seffrid II had to reconstruct the clerestory and put up stone vaulting. He was also responsible for the retro-choir. Between 1245 and 1280 a number of chapels, arranged, as the custom was, round the sides of the cathedral, were thrown into one to form outer aisles. The upper part of the tower dates from 1247, and the spire, 277 feet high and visible at sea, was rebuilt after its fall in 1861.

were confined in the cathedral destroyed some of the ancient woodwork, but the cathedral was refurnished by Bishop Cosin (1660–72). A combined monastery and nunnery was founded at Ely by Etheldreda, ex-queen of Northumbria, who died as its abbess in 679. In 870 the establishment was broken up by the Danes, but it was reconstructed by King Edgar. In 1083 Abbot Simeon commenced the present minster, and in 1109 Ely was made a bishopric. In the first decade of the twelfth century the choir was completed by Abbot Richard, but in 1235 it was further extended

by Bishop Northwold. In 1322 the choir was partially wrecked by the collapse of the central tower. During the episcopate of Bishop Hotham (1319–37) Alan of Walsingham repaired the damage, constructed the central octagon and erected the lady chapel.

Archbishop Theodore made Hereford a bishopric in 697, and its first stone church was built in 825 by Milfrid, king of Mercia, to enclose the shrine of King Ethelbert, who had been murdered by Offa in 792. The present cathedral was begun in 1072 by Bishop Robert de Lozinga and was finished by

Arn-ld

## BOSHAM, WHERE KING CANUTE WAS ASKED TO STAY THE TIDE

Taking the westward road from Chichester to Portsmouth brings one to Bosham, at the head of one of the creeks of Chichester harbour (top). Bosham claims to be the place where Canute reproved his flattering courtiers, who bade him command the sea to hold back. Bosham church was the scene of a Danish royal funeral when the small daughter of Canute was buried there. The coffin containing her bones was unearthed in 1865, during a restoration and a tile in the entrance to the chancel now marks the spot. Below we see Bosham old mill.

Felton

descent to the Ouse valley
and then sharp undulation
to Haywards Heath. This i
a lovely route, of heathe
and open commons : and a
Wivelsfield, two miles beyon
Haywards Heath, we come t
the widespreading common
of Ditchling and Wivelsfield
Here is the Royal Oak inn
scene in 1734 of an atrociou
murder by a Jew pedlar, on
Jacob Harris, who murdere
the landlord, landlady and
maid. He was duly hange
at Horsham, and his body
as was usual, duly gibbete
by the scene of the crim
The remains of the gibbet
post, called locally " Jacob'
Post," are still on the commor
crested with an iron rooste
like a weather-cock, an
pierced with the date. A

**DITCHLING'S FAMOUS MANOR AND CRAWLEY'S OLD-WORLD INN**    Underw

Henry VIII is said to have made this old manor house one of his numerous gifts to Anne Boleyn. Several other old houses an
thirteenth century church make the village a delightful stage on the way. Crawley is the first town over the Sussex border, com
from London along the Brighton Road. The main street is quaintly divided, the east side being in Crawley parish and the west in Ifi
The tower of the church is fourteenth century. The George is one of the few inns which maintains a sign reaching right across the ro

Frith

## HAUNTS OF ANCIENT PEACE AND MODERN BUSTLE AT EAST GRINSTEAD

Felton

In the coffee-room of the Dorset Arms (top), a favourite with motorists, the walls are hung with old prints and from the back windows Ashdown Forest makes a beautiful view. There are some half-timbered houses to be seen in the town besides its finest possession, the Sackville College, founded by a former Earl of Dorset. The old walls embrace a quadrangle of turf, and within are a chapel, a dining hall, whose fireplace bears the date 1619, and the warden's apartments. The foundation provides for six sisters and five brothers.

D

Whiffin

ANCIENT AND CURIOUS LANDMARKS, NATURAL AND ARTIFICIAL, OF KENT AND SUSSEX

Two and a half miles north-west of the station at Malling, Kent, is the village of Addington where a stone circle (bottom left) may be seen, a rarity in this part of the country. Chiddingstone (bottom right) is two miles to the north-west of Penshurst (p. 98) and celebrated for its "chiding stone." This stands in the grounds of Chiddingstone Castle, and consists of a great block of sandstone which tradition associates with a tribal judgement seat of prehistoric days. Trotterscliff or Trottiscliffe (top left) is a landmark eight miles north-west of Maidstone. Near the village was formerly a palace of the bishops of Rochester. One of the most familiar of the Sussex heights is that of Wolstonbury Beacon (top right), 677 feet high, which is topped by a Neolithic camp.

442

corated. Few objects of ornament show the boration which distinguishes the articles found in ntish burial places. It is impossible to name y considerable number of the sites where heathen glo-Saxon burials have been found. They are rhaps most thickly congregated in the Newmarket strict, along the upper Thames, as at Frilford Berkshire, Brighthampton in Oxfordshire, and irford in Gloucestershire, in the midlands between e upper Nene, the Avon and the Soar, and on the Wolds in the East Riding of York. Two lated burials stand out through the singular richness their grave furniture, one at Broomfield in Essex, d the other at Taplow in Buckinghamshire.

NGLO-SAXON history only becomes continuous with the landing of Augustine, the Roman monk espatched by Pope Gregory the Great for the onversion of the English in 597. Like Hengest nd Horsa in the previous century, he seems to have nded at Ebbsfleet in Thanet. The fact that the ing of Kent gave him a place for a church in Canterury, his chief town, gave to this ancient city an nportance which could not have been foreseen. It as the pope's wish that the archbishop of the outhern English should sit at London, already the hief town in England, but the East Saxons, to vhom London belonged, easily converted, as easily elapsed, and the successors of Augustine remained

Felton

**UNIQUE "HELM" TOWER OF SOMPTING**

From Worthing it is two and a half miles to Sompting, where the church is the only one in England that has a gabled or "helm" roof, characteristic of certain churches in the Rhineland. It was built by the Saxons just before the Conquest.

at Canterbury. Gradually in the seventh century an organized Church arose in England. In one respect its organization departed from the Continental model. In France and Italy the bishop was essentially the bishop of the city within which his throne was placed. In England there were few cities of the Continental type, and most of the earliest Anglo-Saxon bishops sat in remote places.

It is naturally in the ecclesiastical sphere that the most striking remains of Anglo-Saxon antiquity are to be found. In the north, at a very early time, there arose a school of sculptors whose work, still visible in many ornate crosses, forms a notable episode in the history of European art. The greatest illustrations of their power are the crosses still standing at Bewcastle in the north of Cumberland and at Ruthwell in Dumfriesshire. Many other crosses of less supreme but remarkable craftsmanship exist to-day in Anglian territory. Many others are only known from disconnected fragments. It is more difficult to form an opinion as to Anglo-Saxon achievement in the more constructive art of architecture. It was only rarely that a church built in the generations which followed the conversion satisfied men of a later age. Few churches built before 1066 have survived without very material alteration.

The remains of Anglo-Saxon church architecture fall into two main periods, the first extending from the conversion to the ninth century, the second, from

Felton

**A SAXON "FIND" AT BRADFORD-ON-AVON**

Complete examples of Saxon churches are very rare because, in the course of centuries, they were restored or enlarged. The finest is at Bradford-on-Avon. After being forgotten it was restored to religious use, and the first baptism for 800 years took place in 1916.

## THE HEART OF AN OLD TOWN AND THE KEEP OF LEWES CASTLE

As the car runs into East Grinstead the view in the upper photograph presents itself with old houses, meditating over the life of the str
on the right.  At the far end it is to the left we must turn for the road to Brighton and, passing out of the town, we see Sackville Coll
(p. 37) on the left hand.  From here it is about eighteen miles to Lewes—whence we are just over eight miles from Brighton—and we s
view of Lewes castle in the lower photograph.  The ascent to the keep is by a zigzag path among the bushes.

Felton

Underwood

## PICTURESQUE AND HISTORIC LANDMARKS OF DOWNLAND

From this south side of Cuckfield churchyard there is a wonderful view towards the Downs, and Cuckfield's shingled spire on its twelfth century tower is a landmark for miles.  Going south from here the road presently runs very near the railway to Brighton, and passes Patcham, whose mill (top left) stands on the edge of a southward spur of the Downs.  Farther south still, and on the very edge of Brighton's suburb, Preston, we come to Blatchington (bottom), from which we look right over the great town to the Channel, fresh and wide beyond the houses.

# Along the Brighton Road

Clayton, farther on from Ditchling, the route at last joins the main road.

Again resuming that road we come past Lowfield Heath and, crossing the Surrey border, come into Sussex and into the little town, or large village, of Crawley, picturesque with its old George inn, on whose gallows sign, stretching across the road, is the statement that the inn was established in 1615. Leaving Crawley, over the railway station level crossing, the road enters the wooded country of St. Leonard's Forest and, passing by Tilgate and Forest Row, comes to Handcross, where the old Red Lion inn stands at the fork of roads. Here the old main road goes slightly to the left; the once new road (made in 1816) bending to the right, steeply descending Handcross Hill and, going through Bolney and Albourne, rising up through the woods past the moated house of Newtimber, rejoins the main road at Pyecombe. This is part of the route used by the record makers and breakers.

Regaining for the last time the main road at Handcross, we descend to Staplefield Common and, going past Slough Green and Whiteman's Green, with the great Ouse Valley viaduct of the Brighton Railway off to the left, looking like some huge Roman viaduct, we come into the quiet old town of Cuckfield, once very busy in the coaching way. Its very life-blood was drained away when the railway was made two miles east, and a station built at what then was the lonely Haywards Heath, now a prosperous township.

Cuckfield is stately in its quiet old age. At the farther end of it is the romantic park of Cuckfield Place, seat of the Sergisons. Harrison Ainsworth had it in mind for the model of Rookwood in his blood-boltered novel of that name. Notice on the right, at the end of the old lime avenue leading to the mansion, the impressive old gatehouse. This was brought from the dismantled house of Slaugham Place, built in the seventeenth century by the Covert family, near Slaugham.

Passing Anstly Cross, the road comes to the twin modern townlets of St. John's Common and Burgess Hill, built on what were commons until about 1840. From hence the grey misty line of the South Downs opens out gloriously, and we come past Friar's Oak inn and Stonepound to Hassocks, another modern settlement at the spot where a turnpike-gate, Hassocks Gate, once stood. Hassocks, in Sussex phrase, means scrub-woods, or coppices. From this point the ascent of Clayton Hill begins, with the little church of Clayton on the left and the grim castellated entrance to Clayton Tunnel to the right. From the crest of this eminence we descend the southern slope of the South Downs, and come into the country of the "deans," the grassy valleys stretching between this and the coast. Through Pyecombe and Patcham the road comes to its destination by Withdean and Preston. Brighton is entered along the Old Steyne, in full view of the Pavilion, that marine palace created by George IV, the "First Gentleman of Europe."

## AT THE END OF THE BRIGHTON ROAD

Doctors started the evolution of the fishing village of Brighthelmstone into the modern Brighton by ordering patients there for the air, and George IV made it fashionable. He it was who had the Pavilion built—it marks the end of our run from London—in the year 1820, and it cost him nearly a million to do it. At least a faint flavour of the atmosphere which the gay George created still lingers about the town, which can hardly forget him while his fantastic Pavilion remains

SCENES OF ANCIENT INTEREST AT GODSTONE, ON THE OLD ROAD TO BRIGHTON

The road from Purley through the Caterham Valley to Godstone is now called the Eastbourne Road, but was once the main route for Brighton. The " Whyte Harte " (top) claims to have served the need of travellers of this road since the reign of Richard II, and its old outside chimney stack, newly topped, is a feature of the exterior. There is a pleasant village green and a famous pond. The lower view was taken farther down the road and shows the old inn in the distance. Godstone is a corruption of Gatesden.

# The Hastings Road

ere they stood, in this noble situation, overlooking e battlefield, for over four hundred and fifty years, ding with the surrender to Henry the Eighth's mmissioners on May 27, 1538. And now all the ory of Battle Abbey and its pomp and pride have nished away, and it has become a show-place for rious visitors one day in the week. The stately tehouse is its chief relic. A refreshment cottage on e right was once the almonry, a place where pilgrims ere entertained. The actual battlefield extended own into the valley to the south. By taking e side that leads to Catsfield, you may best ppreciate, from the invaders' point of view, the ene of the conflict.

OVER Telham Hill and past Starr's Green and Crowhurst Park we come to a fork of roads, ffering a choice of ways into Hastings. If you would ather go to the St. Leonards end, then keep to the ight, along what is called the New London Road. This eads to some puzzling cross-roads at Baldslow, where lectric tramway lines and a maze of wires dissipate ll effects of rurality. Then succeeds the hilly district

of Silverhill, followed by the not altogether beautiful suburb of Bohemia.

The left-hand route, the Old London Road, is perhaps the better choice, although it is true that tramways inflict this route equally. We pass immediately Holmhurst, the old home of Augustus J. C. Hare, with an old relic of London seen in the meadows on the right—the group of statuary removed from the front of S. Paul's Cathedral in 1893, and replaced by the replica now there. Queen Anne and the attendant emblematic figures representing England, France, the American Colonies and Ireland are all more or less mutilated.

And so down to Ore. The deserted and ruinous old church is off to the right, before we come to the modern suburb. Lengthily, and with ever-increasing steepness, the way goes down, past Halton, and finally reaches Hastings, in the Old Town. There, by All Saints and in the street of the same name, you see something of what Hastings was in former days ; and coming to the shore by the fish market, you see its picturesque side, away from the gay " seaside " developments of the present age.

## OUR JOURNEY'S END: HASTINGS FROM THE EAST HILL

Deep set in a vale between two heights—East Hill and the Castle Hill—the old town at Hastings shows a mass of red roofs. This is the old Cinque Port (see p. 318), and still contrives to preserve its identity despite the comparative hugeness of new Hastings, the modern seaside resort. From our vantage point we can observe the castle (see p. 80) and far below and beyond the two piers and the long curve of Pevensey Bay—where William and his Normans landed—towards Eastbourne.

valley of the Rother and into the village of Roberts-bridge. To the left is Bodiam Castle, built by one of the Dalingridge family. It had never any warlike history. A lovely, lily-grown wide moat completely encircles it, and gives the grey roofless walls and towers an ethereal beauty. The late Lord Curzon purchased the castle for the nation.

FROM Robertsbridge the road ascends arduously to John's Cross, and then goes lonely and gradually rising all the way into Battle, between murmuring pines. A railway level-crossing stands midway. The little town of Battle still lives on William the Conqueror and the Battle of Hastings. Battle Abbey soon began to rise on that field of blood which had witnessed the victory of the Normans and the overthrow of the Saxons. Where Harold had fallen, stricken down agonisingly by an arrow descending from the sky, like the stick of a spent rocket, William caused the high altar of his abbey to be built. The King of England, as he had become, spent money freely on that religious establishment, and it was richly endowed with manors far and near ; and was made the centre of a three miles' circuit exempted from all other jurisdictions, ecclesiastical or civil. The abbots, too, were of the more important mitred kind, who sat in the councils of State. It took twenty-eight years to complete the buildings, and William had been seven years in his grave when they were finally consecrated.

DOWN INTO BATTLE AND ONWARDS TO HOLMHURST

From Lamberhurst we continue southward through Robertsbridge to Battle (bottom). Here there is a market where you may see some fine shorthorns changing hands, but, otherwise, Battle's reputation has always depended on William the Conqueror, who founded the great abbey (see p. 201) here. On goes the road towards Hastings, over Telham Hill (see p. 587), and so by Starr's Green to Holmhurst where is the statue of Queen Anne (top), removed from the front of S. Paul's Cathedral to make way for a new replica in 1893.

Dixon-Scott

## HARD BY THE HASTINGS ROAD: THE LAST TOWER OF SCOTNEY

Coming through Lamberhurst and into Sussex as we pursue the course of the road to Hastings we see some lodge gates on our left. These give access to the grounds in which stands what is left of the castle of the de Scotneys. Like Bodiam, it was built in a pool, formed by damming the waters of a little stream, the Bewt. A small piece of the barbican and the beautiful thirteenth century tower, very French in style with its conical roof, is all that remains. Notice the machicolation (see also p. 295 and cf. illustration in p. 82) round the parapet.

WEST COWES.

NEWPORT & VALLEY OF THE MEDINA.

BLACK GANG CHINE ISLE OF WIGHT

SHANKLIN CHINE.

BONCHURCH POND.

THE NEEDLES—ISLE OF WIGHT.

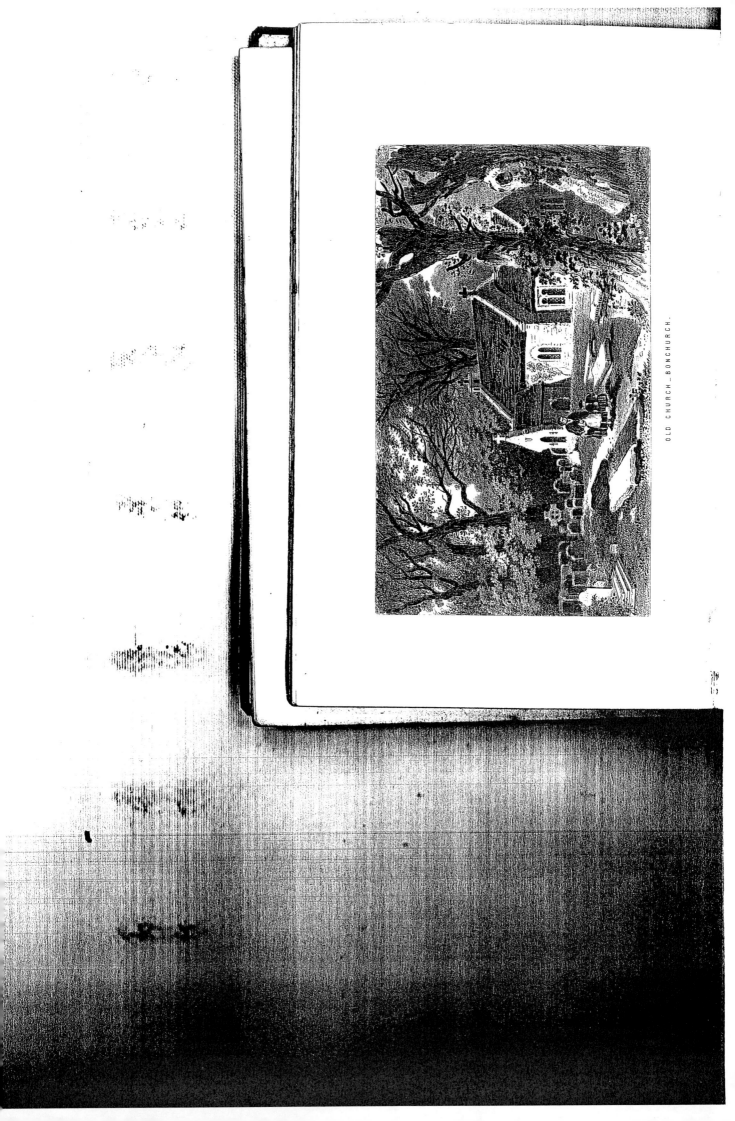

OLD CHURCH — BONCHURCH.

ON THE ISLE OF WIGHT: BEACON TOWERS, S. CATHERINE'S POINT AND QUARR ABBEY

Of these two towers (bottom) that in the foreground was begun but not finished by the Trinity Board in 18th cent., and the other dates from about 1314-28, when a hermit used to tend the light. The modern lighthouse is lower down the hill. Not far from Ryde are the remains of Quarr Abbey, whose name derives from the "quarraria" or quarries in the district, once famous for their building stone. Quarr was founded in 1131 for some Benedictine monks from Normandy, but later became Cistercian. It was dissolved among the lesser religious houses in 1536.

# KENT.

## EXPLANATION.

Market Towns with the Distance from    **DARTFORD**
London in measured Miles, as .......    15

Churches and Chapels ............... +

Turnpike Roads ~~~~~~   *Mail Coach Roads*

Bye Roads ........................

Navigable Canals ................

Rivers ............................

Seats of the Nobility and Gentry ........

N.B. The figures on the Turnpike Roads shew the
distance in measured Miles between the Towns.

CH. DEAL and Walmer send 2 Members Jointly.

E. Div. 182,411. Assesd. Taxes £ 48,597.

W. Div. 206,741. Do. Do.

Scale.

# Along the Pilgrims' Way

**Dell & Wainwright**

**REMAINS OF THE ARCHBISHOPS' PALACE, WROTHAM**

Wrotham, which the Way passes, lies some six miles north-east of Sevenoaks, and is a very ancient place indeed. In Domesday Book it is called Broteham. The house seen above incorporates some of the remains of a palace of the Archbishops of Canterbury, demolished by Archbishop Islip, in Edward III's reign, to complete a manor house at Maidstone.

an interest the more abiding if one thinks of the first makers, back in the dawn of history.

The "Observer," in a leading article (in 1926), when encroachments on the course of the road were threatened, put the whole matter very succinctly : "That the name may be historically vulnerable matters nothing ; the well-known route is among the very oldest of our bequests, furrowed into the map of England long before there was a Canterbury to be its objective, and traversed by the tribe of 'Tegumai' in the days when the man and the wolf were among the wayfarer's first considerations." With that comforting extract we may fitly leave an extremely debatable subject—debatable, that is, for the historian and archaeologist. Of its romantic possibilities there can be no doubt whatever.

"Raygate" stone, which, as its name implies, came from the Reigate area, which incidentally also produced fuller's earth and sand, important minerals in the past. The Pilgrims' Way played its part in the transport of some at least of these materials, but the oft-quoted story that the road was used for the transport of tin is now disproved. No ingots have ever been found along the road, and modern research has shown that the export of tin took place from the Isle of Wight. Not much, therefore, remains of the very circumstantial story with which this account opened. At the most, we may now say that in all probability the road is the survivor of a number of early tracks that followed the hills in Neolithic times, but that it carried any considerable traffic, pilgrim or otherwise, in the Middle Ages is, so far as we know, an unwarranted assumption.

THE fact, then, that much that has been written in the past is picturesque and romantic but improbable is almost certain, but this does not in any way detract from the pleasure to be derived from a leisurely ramble along the Way. The life history of an old road can be studied in all its phases independently of any pilgrims. Here the road has been absorbed into a new concrete "speed-way," there it has been "by-passed" and is rapidly becoming grass-grown. Beyond, it is under the plough, a solitary tree in the midst of a field marking its old course. A little farther it is a sandy lane leading to a ford, after which it is swallowed up in a private park from which the public is excluded. But sufficient remains preserving much of its early character, the elucidating of which is a matter of fascinating interest,

**THE PILGRIMS' GOAL**

Coming along Mercery Lane, Canterbury, in whose narrow way are still the remnants of "The Chequers of Hope," where the pilgrims lodged, one sees, at the far end, Christ Church gateway, which leads to the cathedral and the shrine of S. Thomas.

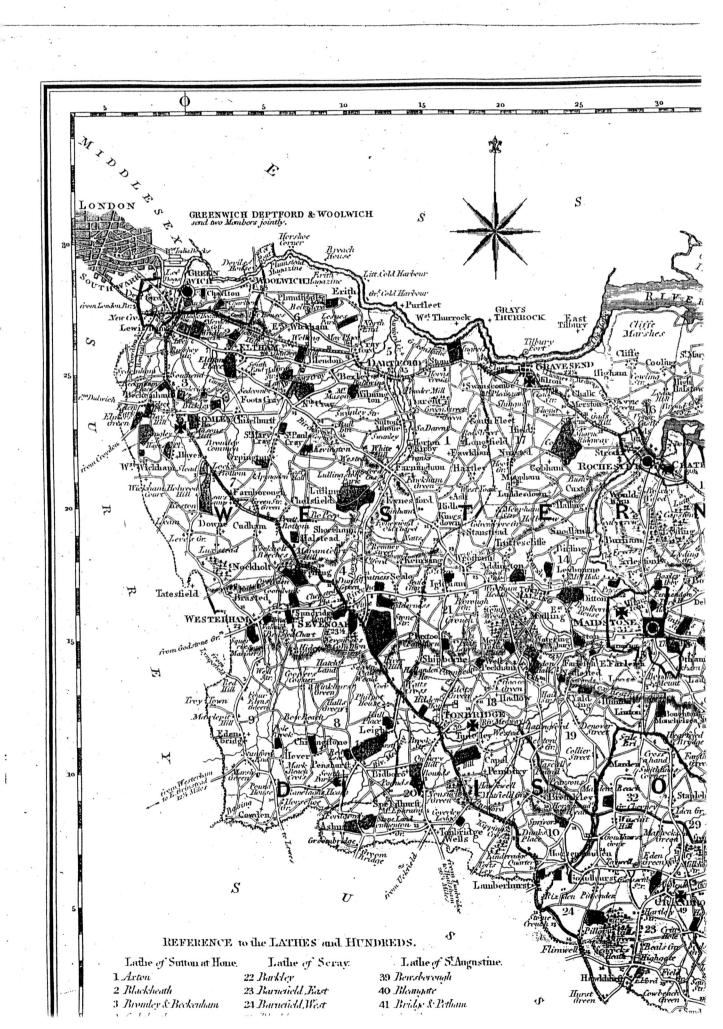

REFERENCE to the LATHES and HUNDREDS.

| Lathe of Sutton at Hone. | Lathe of Scray. | Lathe of St Augustine. |
|---|---|---|
| 1 Axton | 22 Barkley | 39 Bewsborough |
| 2 Blackheath | 23 Barnefield, East | 40 Bleangate |
| 3 Bromley & Beckenham | 24 Barnefield, West | 41 Bridge & Petham |

ROMAN VILLAS AT COLCHESTER AND DARENTH AND THE RECULVER PILLARS AT CANTERBURY

At Colchester is a very fine pavement (bottom). It is situated in Castle Park close to a portion of the city wall for which the Romans were also responsible. Between Dartford and Farningham in Kent is Darenth, where a Roman villa was discovered in 1894–95. The Romans found the climate of Britain chilly, and here (top left and top right) we see the Roman system of central heating, the hypocaust with furnace (left) and the tile supports of the floor. At Canterbury are two pillars from Reculver, said to be Roman, and certainly built in the Roman style.

THE MITRE HOTEL

ST MARY THE VIRGIN (THE UNIVERSITY CHURCH)

THE CAMERA FROM BRASENOSE COLLEGE

GRAMMAR HALL MAGDALEN COLLEGE.

MAGDALEN COLLEGE ＿FER          THE CLOISTERS

THE HIGH
FROM TOP OF MAGDALEN TOWER

THE CAMERA FROM ALL SOULS COLLEGE QUADRANGLE

HOUSES IN ST ALDATES ST

THE DINING HALL CHRISTCHURCH.

QUADRANGLE — ENTRANCE TO DINING HALL, ORIEL.

A QUADRANGLE IN MERTON

THE SUNDIAL
CORPUS
CHRISTI PER

THE RIVER FROM THE FOLLY BRIDGE

OXFORD FROM THE HINKSEY PATH.